DOVER·THRIFT·EDITIONS

The Wit and Wisdom of Abraham Lincoln

A Book of Quotations

ABRAHAM LINCOLN

Edited by Bob Blaisdell

DOVER PUBLICATIONS, INC.
Mineola, New York

GENERAL EDITOR: MARY CAROLYN WALDREP
EDITOR OF THIS VOLUME: BOB BLAISDELL

Copyright

Copyright © 2005 by Dover Publications, Inc.
All rights reserved.

Bibliographical Note

The Wit and Wisdom of Abraham Lincoln is a new work, first published by Dover Publications, Inc., in 2005.

Library of Congress Cataloging-in-Publication Data

Lincoln, Abraham, 1809–1865.
　　The wit and wisdom of Abraham Lincoln / Abraham Lincoln ; edited by Bob Blaisdell.
　　　　p. cm. — (Dover thrift editions)
　　Includes bibliographical references.
　　ISBN-13: 978-0-486-44097-2
　　ISBN-10: 0-486-44097-4
　　1. Lincoln, Abraham, 1809–1865—Quotations. 2. Lincoln, Abraham, 1809–1865—Philosophy. 3. Lincoln, Abraham, 1809–1865—Political and social views. 4. United States—Politics and government—1815–1861—Quotations, maxims, etc. 5. United States—Politics and government—1861–1865—Quotations, maxims, etc. I. Blaisdell, Robert. II. Title. III. Series.

E457.99.B63 2005
973.7'092—dc22

2005041331

Manufactured in the United States by Courier Corporation
44097406
www.doverpublications.com

Note

It is true that while I hold myself without mock modesty the humblest of all individuals that have ever been elevated to the Presidency, I have a more difficult task to perform than any one of them.
—Speech to the New York State Legislature, February 18, 1861

America's most famous and most mythologized man is, even with the myth stripped away, our greatest president and one of our greatest and most representative men. "It is very strange that I," he remarked near the end of the Civil War, "a boy brought up in the woods, and seeing, as it were, but little of the world, should be drifted into the very apex of this great event." How strange (and fortunate), indeed, it was that he, born in 1809 in the backwoods of Kentucky, raised on the frontier of Indiana, a self-educated lawyer in Illinois, found his way to state and then national politics and became, to his own amazement, the president of the United States at its moment of deepest crisis: the secession of rebel states over the issue of the extension of America's most vile institution, slavery. He steered America, "a house divided," as he famously described it, through its war upon itself, its war of brothers and families, and he was assassinated at its end in 1865. Only hours before he was fatally shot, he envisioned the peaceful and healing aftermath of the national and personal devastation, saying to his wife Mary, "We must both be more cheerful in the future. Between the war and the loss of our darling Willie, we have both been very miserable." (One of their young sons had died of disease during the war.)

It is not a myth that Lincoln was wise and witty: his phrasings are alive, quick, clear, and powerful. "It is very common in this country to find great facility of expression and less common to find great lucidity of thought," he told a British journalist. "The combination of the two in one person is very uncommon; but whenever you do find it, you have a great man." Lincoln himself developed that "combination," and he rose to become our "great man." As a public man, he seems to have been generally consistent in his views on slavery, the law, and morality. Though

I have distributed his statements into various broad categories, few of the quotations could not have found an appropriate home in another category or two. I have tried to limit this selection to quotations that were characteristic rather than odd or exceptional and to rely on those statements that were more or less self-explanatory. I have arranged the quotations chronologically within their categories, with the undatable remarks placed thematically. There is, of course, no necessary order in which to read the quotations, though it will become obvious that his statements on any particular topic will be echoed or seconded elsewhere within or outside that category. Many quotations in "Politics and Politicians," for example, are related to those in "The Presidency," "Slavery and the Emancipation Proclamation," and "The War and His Generals," and vice versa.

Almost all the designated "remarks" should be taken as second-hand, but for the most part I have used those recorded by his personal secretaries or by those witnesses deemed fairly reliable. To help me sort out facts from fiction I have depended on the expertise of a handful of the twentieth- and twenty-first century scholars who most thoroughly know Lincoln's views and character: Roy Basler, David Herbert Donald, Don E. Fehrenbacher, Harold Holzer, and Paul M. Zall. The source for the majority of the quotations is the Abraham Lincoln Association's *The Collected Works of Abraham Lincoln*.

During his presidency Lincoln became famous for his jokes and was the purported author of many anecdotes he had never even told, much less created. "I do generally remember a good story when I hear it," he told a friend during the Civil War, "but I never did invent anything original; I am only a retail dealer." He became America's representative of the folksy joke-teller in spite of this, so I have included a few of the jokes he seems to have actually recounted.

While a fine writer, Lincoln was never a good speller, nor did he ever get around to memorizing rules of punctuation. ("With educated people, I suppose, punctuation is a matter of rule; with me it is a matter of feeling," he told a friend in December 1864. "But I must say that I have a great respect for the semicolon; it's a very useful little chap.") For the sake of clarity, I have corrected some of his punctuation and misspellings.

For further reading, I suggest Roy Basler's *Abraham Lincoln: His Speeches and Writings* and *Lincoln,* the excellent biography by David Herbert Donald. Harold Holzer's recent *Lincoln at Cooper Union: The Speech That Made Abraham Lincoln President* is thoroughly interesting.

I thank my father, Dr. F. William Blaisdell, for the loan of his Civil War books and his suggestions of examples of Lincoln's humor, and my son, Max, for help in tagging the hundreds of quotations from *The Collected Works*.

Bibliography and Key to Sources:

Abe Lincoln Laughing: Humorous Anecdotes from Original Sources by and about Abraham Lincoln. Edited by Paul M. Zall. Knoxville, Tennessee: University of Tennessee Press. 1995. [ALL]

"Abe" Lincoln's Yarns and Stories: A Complete Collection of the Funny and Witty Anecdotes That Made Lincoln Famous as America's Greatest Story Teller. Edited by Alexander K. McClure. Philadelphia: Henry Neil. 1901. [YS]

Abraham Lincoln: His Speeches and Writings. Edited by Roy P. Basler. Cleveland, Ohio: World Pub. Co. 1946. [HSW]

The Civil War: A Book of Quotations. Edited by Bob Blaisdell. Mineola, New York: Dover Publications. 2004. [CWBQ]

The Collected Works of Abraham Lincoln. Volumes 1–8. Roy P. Basler, editor. The Abraham Lincoln Association, Springfield, Illinois, and New Brunswick, New Jersey: Rutgers University Press. 1953-1955. [CW1-8]

David Herbert Donald. *Lincoln.* New York: Simon and Schuster. 1995. [DHD]

Great Speeches: Abraham Lincoln. New York: Dover Publications. 1991. [GS]

Harold Holzer. *Lincoln at Cooper Union: The Speech That Made Abraham Lincoln President.* [LCU]

Lincoln as I Knew Him: Gossip, Tributes and Revelations from His Best Friends and Worst Enemies. Edited by Harold Holzer. Chapel Hill, North Carolina: Algonquin Books of Chapel Hill. 1999. [LAIKH]

Recollected Words of Abraham Lincoln. Compiled and edited by Don E. Fehrenbacher and Virginia Fehrenbacher. Stanford, California: Stanford University Press. 1996. [RW]

Contents

AMERICA AND LIBERTY

We find ourselves in the peaceful possession of the fairest portion of earth as regards extent of territory, fertility of soil, and salubrity of climate. We find ourselves under the government of a system of political institutions conducing more essentially to the ends of civil and religious liberty than any of which the history of former times tells us. We, when mounting the stage of existence, found ourselves the legal inheritors of these fundamental blessings. We toiled not in the acquirement of establishment of them—they are a legacy bequeathed us by a *once* hardy, brave, and patriotic but *now* lamented and departed race of ancestors. Theirs was a task (and nobly they performed it) to possess themselves, and through themselves, us, of this goodly land; and to uprear upon its hills and valleys a political edifice of liberty and equal rights; 'tis ours only to transmit these, the former, unprofaned by the foot of an invader; the latter, undecayed by the lapse of time and untorn by usurpation, to the latest generation that fate shall permit the world to know.

—"The Perpetuation of Our Political Institutions": Address before the Young Men's Lyceum of Springfield, Illinois, January 27, 1838 [GS]

❖

At what point shall we expect the approach of danger? By what means shall we fortify against it?—Shall we expect some transatlantic military giant to step the ocean and crush us at a blow? Never!—All the armies of Europe, Asia and Africa combined, with all the treasure of the earth (our own excepted) in their military chest, with a Buonaparte for a commander, could not by force take a drink from the Ohio or make a track on the Blue Ridge in a trial of a thousand years.

At what point then is the approach of danger to be expected? I answer, if it ever reach us, it must spring up amongst us. It cannot come from abroad. If destruction be our lot, we must ourselves be its author and finisher. As a nation of freemen, we must live through all time or die by suicide.

—"The Perpetuation of Our Political Institutions": Address before the Young Men's Lyceum of Springfield, Illinois, January 27, 1838 [HSW]

On the question of liberty, as a principle, we are not what we have been. When we were the political slaves of King George and wanted to be free, we called the maxim that "all men are created equal" a self-evident truth; but now when we have grown fat, and have lost all dread of being slaves ourselves, we have become so greedy to be *masters* that we call the same maxim "a self-evident lie."

—Letter to George Robertson, August 15, 1855 [CW2]

❖

Our progress in degeneracy appears to me to be pretty rapid. As a nation, we began by declaring that "all men *are created equal.*" We now practically read it "all men are created equal, except *negroes.*" . . . When it comes to this I should prefer emigrating to some country where they make no pretense of loving liberty—to Russia, for instance, where despotism can be taken pure, and without the base alloy of hypocrisy.

—Letter to his friend Joshua Speed, August 24, 1855 [HSW]

❖

You can better succeed with the ballot. You can peaceably then redeem the government and preserve the liberties of mankind through your votes and voice and moral influence. . . . Let there be peace. Revolutionize through the ballot box and restore the government once more to the affections and hearts of men by making it express, as it was intended to do, the highest spirit of justice and liberty.

—Speech to Springfield abolitionists, c. 1855 [RW]

❖

We are a great empire. We are eighty years old. We stand at once the wonder and admiration of the whole world, and we must enquire what it is that has given us so much prosperity, and we shall understand that to give up that one thing would be to give up all future prosperity. This cause is that every man can make himself. It has been said that such a race of prosperity has been run nowhere else. . . . we see a people who, while they boast of being free, keep their fellow beings in bondage.

—Speech, Kalamazoo, Michigan, August 27, 1856 [CW2]

❖

As I would not be a *slave*, so I would not be a *master*. This expresses my idea of democracy. Whatever differs from this, to the extent of the difference, is not democracy.

—Note, c. August 1858 [HSW]

What constitutes the bulwark of our own liberty and independence? . . . Our reliance is in the love of liberty which God has planted in our bosoms. Our defense is in the preservation of the spirit which prizes liberty as the heritage of all men, in all lands, everywhere. Destroy this spirit, and you have planted the seeds of despotism around your own doors. Familiarize yourselves with the chains of bondage, and you are preparing your own limbs to wear them.

—Speech, Edwardsville, Illinois, September 11, 1858 [CW3]

❖

If the great American people will only keep their temper, on both sides of the line, the troubles will come to an end, and the question which now distracts the country will be settled just as surely as all other difficulties of like character which have originated in this government have been adjusted. Let the people on both sides keep their self-possession, and just as other clouds have cleared away in the time, so will this, and this great nation shall continue to prosper as heretofore.

—Speech, Pittsburgh, Pennsylvania, February 15, 1861 [CW4]

❖

That portion of the earth's surface which is owned and inhabited by the people of the United States is well adapted to be the home of one national family; and it is not well adapted for two or more.

—Annual Message to Congress, December 1, 1862 [GS]

❖

Our national strife springs not from our permanent part; not from the land we inhabit; not from our national homestead. There is no possible severing of this, but would multiply, and not mitigate, evils among us. In all its adaptations and aptitudes, it demands union, and abhors separation. In fact, it would, ere long, force reunion, however much of blood and treasure the separation might have cost.

—Annual Message to Congress, December 1, 1862 [GS]

❖

The resources, advantages, and powers of the American people are very great, and they have, consequently, succeeded to equally great responsibilities. It seems to have devolved upon them to test whether a government established on the principles of human freedom can be maintained against an effort to build one upon the exclusive foundation of human bondage.

—Letter to the Workingmen of London, February 2, 1863 [CW6]

Four score and seven years ago our fathers brought forth, on this continent, a new nation, conceived in liberty, and dedicated to the proposition that all men are created equal.

—Gettysburg Address, at the dedication of the cemetery
at Gettysburg, Pennsylvania, November 19, 1863 [HSW]

❖

I am not accustomed to the use of language of eulogy; I have never studied the art of paying compliments to women; but I must say that if all that has been said by orators and poets since the creation of the world in praise of women were applied to the women of America, it would not do them justice for their conduct during this war. I will close by saying, God bless the women of America!

—Speech at the Sanitary Fair, Washington, D.C., March 18, 1864 [CW7]

❖

The world has never had a good definition of the word liberty, and the American people, just now, are much in want of one. We all declare for liberty; but in using the same *word* we do not all mean the same *thing*. With some the word liberty may mean for each man to do as he pleases with himself, and the product of his labor; while with others the same word may mean for some men to do as they please with other men, and the product of other men's labor. Here are two, not only different, but incompatible things, called by the same name—liberty. And it follows that each of the things is, by the respective parties, called by the two different and incompatible names—liberty and tyranny.

—Speech, Sanitary Fair, Baltimore, Maryland, April 18, 1864 [HSW]

❖

Nowhere in the world is presented a government of so much liberty and equality. To the humblest and poorest amongst us are held out the highest privileges and positions. The present moment finds me at the White House, yet there is as good a chance for your children as there was for my father's.

—Speech to 148th Ohio Regiment, August 31, 1864 [CW7]

EDUCATION AND ADVICE
FOR YOUNG PEOPLE

Upon the system of education, not presuming to dictate any plan or system respecting it, I can only say that I view it as the most important subject which we as a people can be engaged in. That every man may receive at least a moderate education, and thereby be enabled to read the histories of his own and other countries, by which he may duly appreciate the value of our free institutions, appears to be an object of vital importance, even on this account alone, to say nothing of the advantages and satisfaction to be derived from all being able to read the scriptures and other works, both of a religious and moral nature, for themselves.
—Letter to the people of Sangamo County, March 9, 1832 [HSW]

❖

I cannot read generally. I never read textbooks, for I have no particular motive to drive and whip me to it. I don't and can't remember such reading.
—Remark to William Herndon, his friend and law partner (no date) [DHD]

❖

When I read aloud two senses catch the idea: first, I see what I read; second, I hear it, and therefore I can remember it better.
—Remark to William Herndon, who asked him,
with annoyance, why he read aloud (no date) [LAIKH]

❖

The way for a young man to rise is to improve himself every way he can, never suspecting that anybody wishes to hinder him. Allow me to assure you that suspicion and jealousy never did help any man in any situation. There may sometimes be ungenerous attempts to keep a young man down; and they will succeed too, if he allows his mind to be diverted from its true channel to brood over the attempted injury. Cast about, and see if this feeling has not injured every person you have ever known to fall into it.

—Letter to William Herndon, July 10, 1848 [CW1]

❖

This habit of uselessly wasting time is the whole difficulty; and it is vastly important to you, and still more so to your children that you should break this habit. It is more important to them, because they have longer to live and can keep out of an idle habit before they are in it; easier than they can get out after they are in.

—Letter to John D. Johnston, his stepbrother, December 24, 1848 [CW2]

❖

I am slow to learn and slow to forget that which I have learned. My mind is like a piece of steel, very hard to scratch anything on it and almost impossible after you get it there to rub it out.

—Remark to his friend Joshua Speed (no date) [RW]

❖

Resolve to be honest at all events; and if, in your own judgment, you cannot be an honest lawyer, resolve to be honest without being a lawyer. Choose some other occupation.

—Notes for a lecture on law, July 1, 1850 [DHD]

❖

I am from home too much of my time for a young man to read law with me advantageously. If you are resolutely determined to make a lawyer of yourself, the thing is more than half done already. It is but a small matter whether you read *with* anybody or not. I did not read with anyone. Get the books, and read and study them till you understand them in their principal features; and that is the main thing. It is of no consequence to be in a large town while you are reading. I read at New Salem, which never had three hundred people living in it. The *books*, and your *capacity* for understanding them, are just the same in all places. . . .

Always bear in mind that your own resolution to succeed is more important than any other one thing.

—Letter to Isham Reavis, November 5, 1855 [CW2]

❖

A capacity and taste for reading gives access to whatever has already been discovered by others. It is the key, or one of the keys, to the already solved problems. And not only so, it gives a relish and facility for successfully pursuing the yet unsolved ones.

> —Speech to the Wisconsin State Agricultural Society,
> Milwaukee, Wisconsin, September 30, 1859 [HSW]

❖

Yours of the 24th asking "the best mode of obtaining a thorough knowledge of the law" is received. The mode is very simple, though laborious and tedious. It is only to get the books, and read, and study them carefully. . . . Work, work, work, is the main thing.

> —Letter to John M. Brockman, September 25, 1860 [CW4]

❖

Your good mother tells me you are feeling very badly in your new situation. Allow me to assure you it is a perfect certainty that you will, very soon, feel better—quite happy—if you only stick to the resolution you have taken to procure a military education. I am older than you, have felt badly myself, and *know* what I tell you is true. Adhere to your purpose and you will soon feel as well as you ever did. On the contrary, if you falter, and give up, you will lose the power of keeping any resolution, and will regret it all your life. Take the advice of a friend, who, though he never saw you, deeply sympathizes with you, and stick to your purpose.

> —Letter to Quintin Campbell, who had recently started at West Point; written
> at the request of Campbell's mother and Lincoln's wife, June 28, 1862 [CW5]

❖

It is with deep grief that I learn of the death of your kind and brave father; and, especially, that it is affecting your young heart beyond what is common in such cases. In this sad world of ours, sorrow comes to all; and, to the young, it comes with bitterest agony, because it takes them unawares. The older have learned to ever expect it. I am anxious to afford some alleviation of your present distress. Perfect relief is not possible, except with time.

> —Letter to Fanny McCullough, December 23, 1862 [HSW]

❖

The advice of a father to his son, "Beware of entrance to a quarrel, but being in, bear it that the opposed may beware of thee," is good, and yet not the best. Quarrel not at all. No man resolved to make the most of himself can spare time for personal contention. Still less can he afford to take all the consequences, including the vitiating of his temper and the loss of self-control. Yield larger things to which you can show no more than equal right; and yield lesser ones, though clearly your own. Better give your path to a dog than be bitten by him in contesting for the right. Even killing the dog would not cure the bite.

—Letter to Captain James Cutts, October 26, 1863 [CW6]

❖

With educated people, I suppose, punctuation is a matter of rule; with me it is a matter of feeling. But I must say that I have a great respect for the semicolon; it's a very useful little chap.

—Remark to Noah Brooks, early December 1864 [RW]

FAMILY AND FRIENDS

How miserably things seem to be arranged in this world. If we have no friends, we have no pleasure; and if we have them, we are sure to lose them and be doubly pained by the loss.

> —Letter to Joshua Speed, February 25, 1842 [HSW]

❖

Say to him that if we could meet now, it is doubtful whether it would not be more painful than pleasant; but that if it be his lot to go now, he will soon have a joyous meeting with many loved ones gone before; and where the rest of us, through the help of God, hope ere long to join them.

> —Letter to John D. Johnston, his stepbrother,
> on Lincoln's father's illness, January 12, 1851 [CW2]

❖

It is my pleasure that my children are free, happy, and unrestrained by parental tyranny. Love is the chain to lock a child to its parent.

> —A common remark made, according to his wife Mary, whenever he was
> "chided or praised" for his indulgence of his children (no date) [LAIKH]

❖

Well, Nicolay, my boy is gone—he is actually gone!

> —Remark to his secretary John Nicolay, on the death
> from disease of Lincoln's son Willie, February 20, 1862 [DHD]

❖

Did you ever dream of some lost friend and feel that you were having a sweet communion with him, and yet have a consciousness that it was not a reality? ... That is the way I dream of my lost boy Willie.

> —Remark on his son Willie, to Colonel Le Grand Cannon (no date) [RW]

Think you better put Tad's pistol away. I had an ugly dream about him.
            —Telegram to his wife, about their son Tad, June 9, 1863 [CW6]

❖

Let him run; there's time enough yet for him to learn his letters and get pokey. Bob was just such a little rascal, and now he is a very decent boy.
            —Remark to Noah Brooks on his boys Robert and Tad (no date) [RW]

❖

Do good to those who hate you and turn their ill will to friendship.
            —Remark to his wife, Mary, when she "talked to him
            about former Secretary of the Treasury Salmon Chase
            and those who did him evil" (no date) [LAIKH]

HIS LIFE AND CHARACTER:
CHILDHOOD TO DEATH

Abraham Lincoln is my name
And with my pen I wrote the same
I wrote in both haste and speed
and left it here for fools to read.

—Verses in his boyhood sum book, c. 1824–1826 [DHD]

❖

Abraham Lincoln
his hand and pen
he will be good but
god knows when.

—Verses in his boyhood sum book, c. 1824–1826 [CW1]

❖

Every man is said to have his peculiar ambition. Whether it be true or
not, I can say for one that I have no other so great as that of being truly
esteemed of my fellow men by rendering myself worthy of their esteem.

—Letter to the people of Sangamo County, March 9, 1832 [HSW]

❖

My childhood home I see again,
And gladden with the view;
And still as mem'ries crowd my brain,
There's sadness in it too.

O memory! thou mid-way world
'Twixt Earth and Paradise,
Where things decayed, and loved ones lost
In dreamy shadows rise.

—Poem, c. February 25, 1846 [CW1]

The piece of poetry of my own which I alluded to ["My childhood home I see again"], I was led to write under the following circumstances. In the fall of 1844, thinking I might aid some to carry the State of Indiana for Mr. Clay, I went into the neighborhood in that State in which I was raised, where my mother and only sister were buried, and from which I had been absent about fifteen years. That part of the country is, within itself, as unpoetical as any spot of the earth; but still, seeing it and its objects and inhabitants aroused feelings in me which were certainly poetry; though whether my expression of those feelings is poetry is quite another question.

—Letter to Andrew Johnston, on his poem, April 18, 1846 [HSW]

❖

When first my father settled here,
'Twas then the frontier line:
The panther's scream filled night with fear
And bears preyed on the swine.

—Poem ["The Bear Hunt"], 1846 [HSW]

❖

Being elected to Congress, though I am very grateful to our friends for having done it, has not pleased me as much as I expected.

—Letter to Joshua Speed, October 22, 1846 [HSW]

❖

By the way, Mr. Speaker, did you know I am a military hero? Yes, sir, in the days of the Black Hawk war [1832], I fought, bled, and came away. Speaking of General Cass's career reminds me of my own. I was not at Stillman's defeat, but I was about as near it as Cass was to Hull's surrender; and, like him, I saw the place very soon afterwards. It is quite certain I did not break my sword, for I had none to break; but I bent a musket pretty badly on one occasion. If Cass broke his sword, the idea is, he broke it in desperation; I bent the musket by accident. If General Cass went in advance of me in picking whortleberries, I guess I surpassed him in charges upon the wild onions. If he saw any live fighting Indians, it was more than I did, but I had a good many bloody struggles with the mosquitoes; and although I never fainted from loss of blood, I can truly say I was often very hungry.

—Speech in the U.S. House of Representatives, July 27, 1848 [GS]

Your note, requesting my "signature with a sentiment," was received and should have been answered long since, but that it was mislaid. I am not a very sentimental man; and the best sentiment I can think of is, that if you collect the signatures of all persons who are no less distinguished than I, you will have a very undistinguishing mass of names.

—Letter to C. U. Schlater, January 5, 1849 [HSW]

❖

Herewith is a little sketch [of autobiography], as you requested. There is not much of it, for the reason, I suppose, that there is not much of me.

—Letter to Jesse Fell, for an article in *Chester* (Pennsylvania) *County Times*, December 20, 1859 [CW3]

❖

If any personal description of me is thought desirable, it may be said I am, in height, six feet, four inches, nearly; lean in flesh, weighing, on average, one hundred and eighty pounds; dark complexion, with coarse black hair, and gray eyes—no other marks or brands recollected.

—Letter to Jesse Fell, for an article in *Chester* (Pennsylvania) *County Times*, December 20, 1859 [CW3]

❖

It was a wild region, with many bears and other wild animals still in the woods. There I grew up. There were some schools, so called; but no qualification was ever required of a teacher, beyond "*readin, writin, and cipherin*," the rule of three. . . . There was absolutely nothing to excite ambition for education. Of course when I came of age I did not know much. Still somehow, I could read, write, and cipher to the rule of three, but that was all. I have not been to school since. The little advance I now have upon this store of education I have picked up from time to time under the pressure of necessity.

—Letter to Jesse Fell, for an article in *Chester* (Pennsylvania) *County Times*, December 20, 1859 [CW3]

❖

I remember how, when a mere child, I used to get irritated when anybody talked to me in a way I could not understand. I don't think I ever got angry at anything else in my life. . . . I could not sleep, though I often tried to, when I got on such a hunt after an idea, until I had caught it; and when I thought I had got it, I was not satisfied until I had repeated it over and over, until I had put it in language plain enough, as I thought, for any boy I knew to comprehend. This was a kind of passion with me, and it has stuck by me; for I am never easy now, when I am handling a thought, till I have bounded it north, and bounded it south, and bounded it east, and bounded it west. . . .

—Conversation with Reverend John Gulliver, March 9, 1860 [LCU]

❖

My dear little Miss,

Your very agreeable letter of the 15th is received.

I regret the necessity of saying I have no daughters. I have three sons— one seventeen, one nine, and one seven years of age. They, with their mother, constitute my whole family.

As to the whiskers, having never worn any, do you not think people would call it a piece of silly affectation if I were to begin it now?

—Letter to Grace Bedell, eleven years old,
who suggested he grow a beard, October 19, 1860 [HSW]

❖

Give our clients to understand that the election of a president makes no change in the firm of Lincoln and Herndon. If I live, I'm coming back sometime, and then we'll go right on practicing law as if nothing had ever happened.

—Remark to his law partner William Herndon, February 1861 [RW]

❖

Here I have lived a quarter of a century, and have passed from a young to an old man. Here my children have been born, and one is buried. I now leave, not knowing when or whether ever I may return, with a task before me greater than that which rested upon Washington. Without the assistance of that Divine Being who ever attended him, I cannot succeed. With that assistance, I cannot fail.

—Speech, on leaving Springfield, Illinois, by train
for Washington, D. C., February 11, 1861 [GS]

❖

If I have one vice, and I can call it nothing else, it is not to be able to say no! Thank God for not making me a woman, but if He had, I suppose He would have made me just as ugly as He did, and no one would ever have tempted me.

—Remark to Egbert Viele, May 1862 [RW]

❖

I long ago made up my mind that if anybody wants to kill me, he will do it. If I wore a shirt of mail and kept myself surrounded by a bodyguard, it would be all the same. There are a thousand ways of getting at a man if it is desirable that he should be killed. Besides, in this case, it seems to me, the man who would come after me would be just as objectionable to my enemies.

—Remark to Noah Brooks, c. Spring 1863 [RW]

❖

Mother has got a notion into her head that I shall be assassinated, and to please her I take a cane when I go over to the War Department at nights—when I don't forget it.

—Remark on his wife Mary's concern, to Noah Brooks, c. Spring 1863 [RW]

❖

Common looking people are the best in the world; that is the reason the Lord makes so many of them.

—Recounting, to his secretary John Hay, a remark
made in his dream, December 23, 1863 [ALL]

❖

I was once accosted . . . by a stranger, who said, "Excuse me, sir, but I have an article in my possession which belongs to you." "How is that?" I asked, considerably astonished. The stranger took a jackknife from his pocket. "This knife," said he, "was placed in my hands some years ago with the injunction that I was to keep it until I found a man uglier than myself. I have carried it from that time to this. Allow me to say, sir, that I think you are fairly entitled to the property."

—Anecdote about the period when Lincoln practiced law on the Illinois
State circuit, told to his portrait painter Francis Carpenter, 1864 [RW]

❖

It is very strange that I, a boy brought up in the woods, and seeing, as it were, but little of the world, should be drifted into the very apex of this great event.

—Remark to Josiah Blackburn, c. late July 1864 [RW]

❖

It is a little singular that I, who am not a vindictive man, should have always been before the people for election in canvases marked for their bitterness—always but once; when I came to Congress [1846] it was a quiet time. But always besides that, the contests in which I have been prominent have been marked with great rancor.

—Remark to his secretary John Hay on election day, November 8, 1864 [RW]

I cannot bring myself to believe that any human being lives who would do me any harm.

>   —Remark about a reported threat on his life on the day
>   he arrived in Richmond, Virginia, April 4, 1865 [DHD]

❖

Creswell, old fellow, everything is bright this morning. The war is over. It has been a tough time, but we have lived it out. Or some of us have.

>   —In conversation to Senator John Creswell of Maryland,
>   April 14, 1865 [CWBQ]

❖

We must both be more cheerful in the future. Between the war and the loss of our darling Willie, we have both been very miserable.

>   —Remark to his wife Mary, April 14, 1865. (One of their sons
>   had died of disease in 1862. On this night the Lincolns
>   went to the theater, and the President was shot.) [CWBQ]

LAW AND THE CONSTITUTION

When men take it in their heads today to hang gamblers or burn murderers, they should recollect that, in the confusion usually attending such transactions, they will be as likely to hang or burn someone who is neither a gambler nor a murderer as one who is; and that, acting upon the example they set, the mob of tomorrow may, and probably will, hang or burn some of them by the very same mistake.

—"The Perpetuation of Our Political Institutions": Address before the Young Men's Lyceum of Springfield, Illinois, January 27, 1838 [HSW]

❖

... by the operation of the mobocratic spirit, which all must admit is now abroad in the land, the strongest bulwark of any Government, and particularly of those constituted like ours, may effectually be broken down and destroyed—I mean the *attachment* of the People. ... whenever the vicious portion of population shall be permitted to gather in bands of hundreds and thousands, and burn churches, ravage and rob provision-stores, throw printing presses into rivers, shoot editors, and hang and burn obnoxious persons at pleasure, and with impunity; depend on it, this Government cannot last.

—"The Perpetuation of Our Political Institutions": Address before the Young Men's Lyceum of Springfield, Illinois, January 27, 1838 [HSW]

❖

As the patriots of '76 did to the support of the Constitution and laws, let every American pledge his life, his property, and his sacred honor; let every man remember that to violate the law is to trample on the blood of his father and to tear the character of his own and his children's liberty.

—"The Perpetuation of Our Political Institutions": Address before the Young Men's Lyceum of Springfield, Illinois, January 27, 1838 [HSW]

How effectual have penitentiaries heretofore been in preventing the crimes they were established to suppress? Has not confinement in them long been the legal penalty of larceny, forgery, robbery, and many other crimes, in almost all the states? And yet, are not those crimes committed weekly, daily, nay, and even hourly in every one of those states? Again, the gallows has long been the penalty of murder, and yet we scarcely open a newspaper that does not relate a new case of crime. If, then, the penitentiary has *heretofore* failed to prevent larceny, forgery and robbery, and the gallows and halter have likewise failed to prevent murder, by what process of reasoning, I ask, is it that we are to conclude the penitentiary will hereafter prevent the stealing of the public money?

—Speech, Hall of the House of Representatives,
Springfield, Illinois, December 26, 1839 [HSW]

❖

There is a vague popular belief that lawyers are necessarily dishonest. I say vague, because when we consider to what extent confidence and honors are reposed in and conferred upon lawyers by the people, it appears improbable that their impression of dishonesty is very distinct and vivid. Yet the impression is common, almost universal.

—Notes for a lecture on law, c. July 1850 [CW2]

❖

I dare not trust this case on presumptions that this court knows all things. I argued the case on the presumption that the court did not know any thing.

—Remark to William Herndon (no date) [DHD]

❖

. . . if all men were just, there still would be *some*, though not *so much*, need of government.

—Note for a lecture, c. July 1, 1854 [CW2]

❖

When the white man governs himself that is self-government; but when he governs himself and also governs *another* man, that is *more* than self-government—that is despotism.

—Speech, Peoria, Illinois, October 16, 1854 [HSW]

❖

. . . no man is good enough to govern another man *without that other's consent.*

—Speech, Peoria, Illinois, October 16, 1854 [HSW]

So far as peaceful, voluntary emancipation is concerned, the condition of the negro slave in America, scarcely less terrible to the contemplation of a free mind, is now as fixed and hopeless of change for the better as that of the lost souls of the finally impenitent. The Autocrat of all the Russias will resign his crown and proclaim his subjects free republicans sooner than will our American masters voluntarily give up their slaves.

—Letter to George Robertson, August 15, 1855 [CW2]

❖

In your assumption that there may be a fair decision of the slavery question in Kansas, I plainly see you and I would differ about the Nebraska law. I look upon that enactment not as a *law*, but as *violence* from the beginning. It was conceived in violence, passed in violence, is maintained in violence, and is being executed in violence.

—Letter to Joshua Speed, August 24, 1855 [HSW]

❖

All the powers of earth seem rapidly combining against him. . . . They have him in his prison house; they have searched his person, and left no prying instrument with him. One after another they have closed the heavy iron doors upon him, and now they have him, as it were, bolted in with a lock of a hundred keys, which can never be unlocked without the concurrence of every key; the keys in the hands of a hundred different men, and they scattered to a hundred different and distant places, and they stand musing as to what invention, in all the dominions of mind and matter, can be produced to make the impossibility of his escape more complete than it is.

—Speech, Springfield, Illinois, June 26, 1857 [CW2]

❖

I am for the people of the whole nation doing just as they please in all matters which concern the whole nation; for those of each part doing just as they choose in all matters which concern no other part; and for each individual doing just as he chooses in all matters which concern nobody else. This is the principle. Of course I am content with any exception which the Constitution or the actually existing state of things makes a necessity. But neither the principle nor the exception will admit the indefinite spread and perpetuity of human slavery.

—Draft of a speech, c. May 18, 1858 [CW2]

❖

A man cannot prove a negative, but he has a right to claim that when a man makes an affirmative charge, he must offer some proof to show the truth of what he says. I certainly cannot introduce testimony to show the negative about things, but I have a right to claim that if a man says he *knows* a thing, then he must show *how* he knows it. I always have a right to claim this, and it is not satisfactory to me that he may be "conscientious" on the subject.

—First debate with Stephen Douglas, Ottawa, Illinois, August 21, 1858 [CW3]

❖

... there is no reason in the world why the negro is not entitled to all the natural rights enumerated in the Declaration of Independence, the right to life, liberty and the pursuit of happiness.

—First debate with Stephen Douglas, Ottawa, Illinois, August 21, 1858 [CW3]

❖

With public sentiment, nothing can fail; without it, nothing can succeed. Consequently, he who molds public sentiment goes deeper than he who enacts statutes or pronounces decisions. He makes statutes and decisions possible or impossible to be executed.

—First debate with Stephen Douglas, Ottawa, Illinois, August 21, 1858 [CW3]

❖

What is Popular Sovereignty? Is it the right of the people to have slavery or not have it, as they see fit, in the territories? I will state—and I have an able man to watch me—my understanding is that Popular Sovereignty, as now applied to the question of slavery, does allow the people of a Territory to have slavery if they want to, but does not allow them *not* to have it if they *do not* want it.

—First debate with Stephen Douglas, Ottawa, Illinois, August 21, 1858 [CW3]

❖

... the institution of slavery is only mentioned in the Constitution of the United States two or three times, and in neither of these cases does the word "slavery" or "negro" occur; but covert language is used each time, and for a purpose full of significance. ... and that purpose was that in our Constitution, which it was hoped and is still hoped will endure forever— when it should be read by intelligent and patriotic men, after the institution of slavery had passed from among us—there should be nothing on the face of the great charter of liberty suggesting that such a thing as negro slavery had ever existed among us.

—Seventh debate with Stephen Douglas, Alton, Illinois,
October 15, 1858 [CW3]

It is not true that our fathers, as Judge Douglas assumes, made this government part slave and part free. Understand the sense in which he puts it. He assumes that slavery is a rightful thing within itself—was introduced by the framers of the Constitution. The exact truth is that they found the institution existing among us, and they left it as they found it. But in making the government they left this institution with many clear marks of disapprobation upon it. They found slavery among them and they left it among them because of the difficulty—the absolute impossibility of its immediate removal.

—Seventh debate with Stephen Douglas, Alton, Illinois, October 15, 1858 [CW3]

❖

This is a world of compensations; and he who would be no slave must consent to have no slave. Those who deny freedom to others deserve it not for themselves; and, under a just God, cannot long retain it.

—Letter to H. L. Pierce and others, April 6, 1859 [HSW]

❖

We want, and must have, a national policy as to slavery which deals with it as being a wrong.

—Notes for his speeches at Columbus and Cincinnati, Ohio, September 16–17, 1859 [CW3]

❖

To correct the evils, great and small, which spring from want of sympathy and from positive enmity among *strangers*, as nations or as individuals, is one of the highest functions of civilization.

—Speech to the Wisconsin State Agricultural Society, Milwaukee, Wisconsin, September 30, 1859 [HSW]

❖

May I beg of you to consider the difficulties of my position and solicit your kind assistance in it? Our security in the seizing of arms for our destruction will amount to nothing at all if we are never to make mistakes in searching a place where there are none. I shall continue to do the very best I can to discriminate between *true* and *false* men. In the mean time, let me, once more, beg your assistance in allaying irritations which are unavoidable.

—Letter to "unidentified persons," c. September 15, 1861 [CW4]

Had slavery no existence among us, and were the question asked shall we adopt such an institution, we should agree as to the reply which should be made. If there be any diversity in our views it is not as to whether we should receive slavery when free from it, but as to how we may best get rid of it already amongst us. Were an individual asked whether we would wish to have a wen on his neck, he could not hesitate as to the reply; but were it asked whether a man who has such a wen should at once be relieved of it by the application of a surgeon's knife, there might be diversity of opinion, perhaps the man might bleed to death as the result of such an operation.

> —Speech to a committee from the Synod of the
> Reformed Presbyterian Church, July 17, 1862 [CW5]

❖

The traitor against the general government forfeits his slave, at least as justly as he does any other property; and he forfeits both to the government against which he offends. The government, so far as there can be ownership, thus owns the forfeited slaves; and the question for Congress, in regard to them, is, "Shall they be made free, or be sold to new masters?" I perceive no objection to Congress deciding in advance that they shall be free.

> —Message to the 37th Congress, Second Session, July 17, 1862 [CW5]

❖

Long experience has shown that armies cannot be maintained unless desertion shall be punished by the severe penalty of death. The case requires, and the law and the Constitution sanction, this punishment. Must I shoot a simple-minded soldier boy who deserts while I must not touch a hair of a wily agitator who induces him to desert? This is none the less injurious when effected by getting a father, or brother, or friend into a public meeting, and there working upon his feelings till he is persuaded to write the soldier boy that he is fighting in a bad cause, for a wicked administration of a contemptible government, too weak to arrest and punish him if he shall desert. I think that in such a case to silence the agitator and save the boy is not only constitutional, but, withal, a great mercy.

> —Letter to Erastus Corning and others, June 12, 1863 [HSW]

❖

. . . the Constitution is not in its application in all respects the same in cases of rebellion or invasion involving the public safety as it is in times of profound peace and public security. The Constitution itself makes the distinction, and I can no more be persuaded that the government can constitutionally take no strong measures in time of rebellion, because it can be shown that the same could not be lawfully taken in time of peace, than I can be persuaded that a particular drug is not good medicine for a sick man because it can be shown to not be good food for a well one.

—Letter to Erastus Corning and others, June 12, 1863 [HSW]

❖

Was it possible to lose the nation, and yet preserve the Constitution? By general law, life and limb must be protected; yet often a limb must be amputated to save a life; but a life is never wisely given to save a limb. I felt that measures, otherwise unconstitutional, might become lawful by becoming indispensable to the preservation of the Constitution through the preservation of the nation. Right or wrong, I assumed this ground, and now avow it. I could not feel that, to the best of my ability, I had even tried to preserve the Constitution if, to save slavery, or any minor matter, I should permit the wreck of government, country, and Constitution all together.

—Remarks to Kentucky Governor Thomas Bramlette,
Frankfort Commonwealth editor Albert Hodges,
and Senator Archibald Dixon, March 26, 1864 [CW7]

❖

Neither slavery nor involuntary servitude, except as a punishment for crime whereof the party shall have been duly convicted, shall exist within the United States, or any place subject to their jurisdiction.

—Submission of "a proposition to amend the Constitution of the
United States," the 13th Amendment, February 1, 1865 [CW8]

❖

A man who denies to other men equality of rights is hardly worthy of freedom; but I would give even to him all the rights which I claim for myself.

—Remark to his secretary John Hay, April 1865 [RW]

POLITICS AND POLITICIANS

My politics are short and sweet, like the old woman's dance.
>—Speech while campaigning for the Illinois State Legislature,
>in Pappsville, 1832 [RW]

❖

These capitalists generally act harmoniously and in concert to fleece the people, and now that they have got into a quarrel with themselves, we are called upon to appropriate the people's money to settle the quarrel.
>—Speech in the Illinois Legislature, January 11, 1837 [HSW]

❖

Mr. Chairman, this work is exclusively the work of politicians, a set of men who have interests aside from the interests of the people, and who, to say the most of them, are, taken as a mass, at least one long step removed from honest men. I say this with the greater freedom, because, being a politician myself, none can regard it as personal.
>—Speech in the Illinois Legislature, January 11, 1837 [HSW]

❖

The *probability* that we may fall in the struggle ought not to deter us from the support of a cause we believe to be just; it *shall not* deter me. If ever I feel the soul within me elevate and expand to those dimensions not wholly unworthy of its Almighty Architect, it is when I contemplate the cause of my country deserted by all the world beside, and I standing up boldly and alone and hurling defiance at her victorious oppressors. Here, without contemplating consequences, before High Heaven, and in the face of the world, I swear eternal fidelity to the just cause, as I deem it, of the land of my life, my liberty and my love. And who, that thinks with me, will not fearlessly adopt the oath that I take? Let none falter who thinks he is right, and we may succeed. But if, after all, we shall fail, be it so. We still shall have the proud consolation of saying to our consciences, and to the departed shade of our country's freedom, that the cause approved of our judgment, and adored of our hearts, in disaster, in chains, in torture, in death, we *never* faltered in defending.

—Speech, Hall of the House of Representatives, Springfield, Illinois, December 26, 1839 [HSW]

❖

"We are not to do *evil* that good may come." This general proposition is doubtless correct; but did it apply? If by your votes you could have prevented the *extension* of slavery, would it not have been *good* and not *evil* to have used your votes, even though it involved the casting of them for a slave-holder? By the *fruit* of the tree is to be known. An *evil* tree cannot bring forth *good* fruit. If the fruit of electing Mr. Clay would have been to prevent the extension of slavery, could the act of electing him have been *evil*?

—Letter to Williamson Durley, an abolitionist, October 3, 1845 [CW1]

❖

It is certain that struggles between candidates do not strengthen a party; but who are most responsible for these struggles, those who are willing to live and let live, or those who are resolved, at all hazards, to take care of "number one"?

—Letter to John Hardin, February 7, 1846 [CW1]

❖

When the war began, it was my opinion that all those who, because of knowing too little, or because of knowing too much, could not conscientiously approve the conduct of the President (in the beginning of it), should, nevertheless, as good citizens and patriots remain silent on that point, at least till the war should be ended.

—Speech on the war with Mexico, U.S. House of Representatives, January 12, 1848 [CW1]

❖

. . . I more than suspect already that he [President James K. Polk] is deeply conscious of being in the wrong; that he feels the blood of this war, like the blood of Abel, is crying to Heaven against him; that he ordered General Taylor into the midst of a peaceful Mexican settlement, purposely to bring on a war; that originally having some strong motive—what I will not stop now to give my opinion concerning—to involve the two countries in a war, and trusting to escape scrutiny by fixing the public gaze upon the exceeding brightness of military glory—that attractive rainbow that rises in showers of blood—that serpent's eye that charms to destroy—he plunged into it, and has swept *on* and *on*, till, disappointed in his calculation of the ease with which Mexico might be subdued, he now finds himself he knows not where.

—Speech on the war with Mexico, U.S. House of Representatives,
January 12, 1848 [HSW]

❖

. . . it is a singular omission in this message that it nowhere intimates *when* the President expects the war to terminate. At its beginning, General Scott was, by this same President, driven into disfavor, if not disgrace, for intimating that peace could not be conquered in less than three or four months. But now, at the end of about twenty months, during which time our arms have given us the most splendid successes—every department, and every part, land and water, officers and privates, regulars and volunteers, doing all that men *could* do, and hundreds of things which it had ever before been thought men could *not* do—after all this, this same President gives us a long message without showing us that, *as to the end*, he himself has even an imaginary conception. As I have before said, he knows not where he is. He is a bewildered, confounded, and miserably perplexed man. God grant he may be able to show there is not something about his conscience more painful than all his mental perplexity!

—Speech to the U.S. House of Representatives on the Mexican War,
January 12, 1848 [CW1]

❖

Allow the President to invade a neighboring nation whenever *he* shall deem it necessary to repel an invasion, and you allow him to do so *whenever he may choose to say* he deems it necessary for such purpose—and you allow him to make war at pleasure.

—Letter to William H. Herndon, February 15, 1848 [HSW]

❖

I protest against your calling the condemnation of Polk "opposing the war." In thus assuming that all must be opposed to the war, even though they vote supplies, who do not endorse Polk, with due deference I say I think you fall into one of the artfully set traps of Locofocoism.

—Letter to Usher Linder, March 22, 1848 [CW1]

❖

That the Constitution gives the President a negative on legislation, all know; but that this negative should be so combined with platforms and other appliances as to enable him and, in fact, almost compel him to take the whole of legislation into his own hands is what we object to—is what General Taylor objects to—and is what constitutes the broad distinction between you and us.

—Speech in the U.S. House of Representatives, July 27, 1848 [GS]

❖

I understand your idea, that if a Presidential candidate avow his opinion upon a given question, or rather upon all questions, and the people, with full knowledge of this, elect him, they thereby distinctly approve all those opinions. This, though plausible, is a most pernicious deception.

—Speech in the U.S. House of Representatives, July 27, 1848 [GS]

❖

A fellow once advertised that he had made a discovery by which he could make a new man out of an old one, and have enough of the stuff left to make a little yellow dog. Just such a discovery has General Jackson's popularity been to you. You not only twice made President of him out of it, but you have had enough of the stuff left to make Presidents of several comparatively small men since; and it is your chief reliance now to make still another.

—Speech in the U.S. House of Representatives, July 27, 1848 [GS]

❖

Mr. Speaker, we have all heard of the animal standing in doubt between two stacks of hay and starving to death; the like of that would never happen to General Cass. Place the stacks a thousand miles apart, he would stand stock-still midway between them and eat them both at once; and the green grass along the line would be apt to suffer some too, at the same time. By all means, make him President, gentlemen. He will feed you bounteously—if—if there is any left after he shall have helped himself.

—Speech in the U.S. House of Representatives, July 27, 1848.
(Lincoln had analyzed Cass's accounts from 1813–1831
when he was Governor of Michigan Territory, wherein Cass
made daily-expense claims from various places.) [GS]

❖

The declaration that we have always opposed the war is true or false, accordingly as one may understand the term "opposing the war." If to say "the war was unnecessarily and unconstitutionally commenced by the President," be opposing the war, then the Whigs have very generally opposed it.

—Speech in the U.S. House of Representatives, July 27, 1848 [GS]

Repeal the Missouri Compromise—repeal all compromises—repeal the Declaration of Independence—repeal all past history, you still cannot repeal human nature. It still will be the abundance of man's heart that slavery extension is wrong; and out of the abundance of his heart, his mouth will continue to speak.

—Speech, Peoria, Illinois, October 16, 1854 [HSW]

❖

Near eighty years ago we began by declaring that all men are created equal; but now from that beginning we have run down to the other declaration, that for *some* men to enslave others is a "sacred right of self-government." These principles cannot stand together. They are as opposite as God and Mammon; and whoever holds to the one must despise the other.

—Speech, Peoria, Illinois, October 16, 1854 [HSW]

❖

Stand with anybody that stands *right*. Stand with him while he is right and *part* with him when he goes wrong.

—Speech, Peoria, Illinois, October 16, 1854 [HSW]

❖

Although in a private letter or conversation you will express your preference that Kansas shall be free, you would vote for no man for Congress who would say the same thing publicly.... The slave-breeders and slave-traders are a small, odious and detested class among you; and yet in politics, they dictate the course of all of you, and are as completely your masters as you are the master of your own negroes.

—Letter to Joshua Speed, August 24, 1855 [HS]

❖

The Republicans inculcate, with whatever of ability they can, that the negro is a man; that his bondage is cruelly wrong, and that the field of his oppression ought not to be enlarged. The Democrats deny his manhood; deny, or dwarf to insignificance, the wrong of his bondage; so far as possible crush all sympathy for him, and cultivate and excite hatred and disgust against him; compliment themselves as Union-savers for doing so; and call the indefinite outspreading of his bondage "a sacred right of self-government."

—Speech, Springfield, Illinois, June 26, 1857 [CW2]

Whether the Lecompton constitution should be accepted or rejected is a question upon which, in the minds of men not committed to any of its antecedents, and controlled only by the Federal Constitution, by republican principles, and by a sound morality, it seems to me there could not be two opinions. It should be throttled and killed as hastily and as heartily as a rabid dog.

—Draft of a speech, c. May 18, 1858 [CW2]

❖

Welcome, or unwelcome, agreeable, or disagreeable, whether this shall be an entire slave nation *is* the issue before us. Every incident—every little shifting of scenes or of actors—only clears away the intervening trash, compacts and consolidates the opposing hosts, and brings them more and more distinctly face to face. The conflict will be a severe one; and it will be fought through by those who *do* care for the result, and not by those who do not care—by those who are for and those who are against a legalized national slavery.

—Draft of a speech, c. May 18, 1858 [CW2]

❖

A house divided against itself cannot stand.

I believe this government cannot endure, permanently half *slave* and half *free*.

I do not expect the Union to be *dissolved*—I do not expect the house to *fall*—but I *do* expect it will cease to be divided.

It will become *all* one thing or *all* the other.

—Speech accepting the nomination for U.S. Senator, Republican
State Convention, Springfield, Illinois, June 16, 1858 [GS]

❖

You can fool some of the people all of the time, and all of the people some of the time, but you can't fool all of the people all of the time.

—Attributed to Lincoln, but never contemporaneously quoted,
during his Bloomington, Illinois, speech on May 29, 1856 [ALL]

❖

The difference between the Republican and the Democratic parties on the leading issues of this contest, as I understand it, is that the former consider slavery a moral, social and political wrong, while the latter *do not* consider it either a moral, social or political wrong; and the action of each, as respects the growth of the country and the expansion of our population, is squared to meet these views.

—Speech, Edwardsville, Illinois, September 11, 1858 [HSW]

The Republican party . . . hold that this government was instituted to secure the blessings of freedom, and that slavery is an unqualified evil to the negro, to the white man, to the soil, and to the State.

—Speech, Edwardsville, Illinois, September 11, 1858 [HSW]

❖

It is worthwhile to observe that we have generally had comparative peace upon the slavery question and that there has been no cause for alarm until it was excited by the effort to spread it into new territory. Whenever it has been limited to its present bounds and there has been no effort to spread it, there has been peace. All the trouble and convulsion has proceeded from efforts to spread it over more territory.

—Third debate with Stephen Douglas, September 15, 1858 [CW3]

❖

. . . there is a sentiment in the country contrary to me—a sentiment which holds that slavery is not wrong, and therefore it goes for policy that does not propose dealing with it as a wrong. That policy is the Democratic policy, and that sentiment is the Democratic sentiment. . . . Perhaps the Democrat who says he is as much opposed to slavery as I am will tell me that I am wrong about this. I wish him to examine his own course in regard to this matter a moment, and then see if his opinion will not be changed a little. You say it is wrong; but don't you constantly object to anybody else saying so? Do you not constantly argue that this is not the right place to oppose it? You say it must not be opposed in the free States, because slavery is not here; it must not be opposed in the slave States, because it is there; it must not be opposed in politics, because that will make a fuss; it must not be opposed in the pulpit, because it is not religion. Then where is the place to oppose it? There is no suitable place to oppose it. There is no place in the country to oppose this evil overspreading the continent, which you say yourself is coming.

—Sixth debate with Stephen Douglas, Quincy, Illinois,
October 13, 1858 [CW3]

❖

To the best of my judgment I have labored *for* and not *against* the Union. As I have not felt, so I have not expressed any harsh sentiment towards our Southern brethren. I have constantly declared, as I really believed, the only difference between them and us is the difference of circumstances.

—Speech, Springfield, Illinois, October 30, 1858 [HSW]

The [Democrats] of today hold the *liberty* of one man to be absolutely nothing when in conflict with another man's right of *property*. Republicans, on the contrary, are for both the *man* and the *dollar*, but in cases of conflict, the man *before* the dollar.

—Letter to H. L. Pierce and others, April 6, 1859 [HSW]

❖

... it is now no child's play to save the principles of Jefferson from total overthrow in this nation.

One would start with great confidence that he could convince any sane child that the simpler propositions of Euclid are true; but, nevertheless, he would fail, utterly, with one who should deny the definitions of axioms. The principles of Jefferson are the definitions and axioms of free society.

—Letter to H. L. Pierce and others, April 6, 1859 [HSW]

❖

I have said that in our present moral tone and temper, we are strong enough for our open enemies; and so we are. But the chief effect of Douglasism is to change that tone and temper. Men who support the measures of a political leader do, almost of necessity, adopt the reasoning and sentiments the leader advances in support of them.

—Notes for his speeches at Columbus and Cincinnati, Ohio, September 16–17, 1859 [CW3]

❖

If I might advise my Republican friends here, I would say to them, leave your Missouri neighbors alone. Have nothing whatever to do with their slaves. Have nothing whatever to do with the white people, save in a friendly way. Drop past differences, and so conduct yourselves that if you cannot be at peace with them, the fault shall be wholly theirs.

—Speech, Leavenworth, Kansas, December 3, 1859 [CW3]

❖

... you [Democrats] are for the Union; and you greatly fear the success of the Republicans would destroy the Union. Why? Do the Republicans declare against the Union? Nothing like it. Your own statement of it is that if the Black Republicans elect a President, you won't stand it. You will break up the Union. That will be your act, not ours. To justify it, you must show that our policy gives you just cause for such desperate action. Can you do that? When you attempt it, you will find that our policy is exactly the policy of the men who made the Union. Nothing more and nothing less.

—Speech, Leavenworth, Kansas, December 3, 1859 [CW3]

Old John Brown has just been executed for treason against a state. We cannot object, even though he agreed with us in thinking slavery wrong. That cannot excuse violence, bloodshed, and treason. It could avail him nothing that he might think himself right. So, if constitutionally we elect a President, and therefore you undertake to destroy the Union, it will be our duty to deal with you as old John Brown has been dealt with. We shall try to do our duty. We hope and believe that in no section will a majority so act as to render such extreme measures necessary.

> —Speech, Leavenworth, Kansas, December 3, 1859 [CW3]

❖

The fact that we get no votes in your section is a fact of your making, and not of ours. And if there be fault in that fact, that fault is primarily yours, and remains until you show that we repel you by some wrong principle or practice.

> —Speech (the "a few words to the Southern people" section) at the
> Cooper Union Institute, New York City, February 27, 1860 [CWBQ]

❖

If slavery is right, all words, acts, laws, and constitutions against it are themselves wrong, and should be silenced, and swept away. If it is right, we cannot justly object to its nationality—its universality; if it is wrong, they cannot justly insist upon its extension—its enlargement. All they ask, we could readily grant, if we thought slavery right; all we ask, they could as readily grant, if they thought it wrong. Their thinking it right, and our thinking it wrong, is the precise fact upon which depends the whole controversy. Thinking it right, as they do, they are not to blame for desiring its full recognition, as being right; but, thinking it wrong, as we do, can we yield to them? Can we cast our votes with their view, and against our own? In view of our moral, social, and political responsibilities, can we do this?

> —Speech at the Cooper Union Institute, New York City,
> February 27, 1860 [GS]

❖

The new Territories are the newly made bed to which our children are to go, and it lies with the nation to say whether they shall have snakes mixed up with them or not. It does not seem as if there could be much hesitation what our policy should be.

> —Speech, New Haven, Connecticut, March 6, 1860 [CW4]

Henry Clay

Mr. Clay's lack of a more perfect early education, however it may be re-
gretted generally, teaches at least one profitable lesson: it teaches that in
this country one can scarcely be so poor but that, if he *will*, he *can* ac-
quire sufficient education to get through the world respectably.

—Eulogy on Henry Clay, the State House, Springfield, Illinois,
July 6, 1852 [HSW]

❖

With other men, to be defeated was to be forgotten; but to him, defeat
was but a trifling incident, neither changing him or the world's estimate
of him. Even those of both political parties who have been preferred to
him for the highest office have run far briefer courses than he, and left
him, still shining, high in the heavens of the political world. Jackson, Van
Buren, Harrison, Polk, and Taylor all rose *after* and set long before him.

—Eulogy on Henry Clay, the State House, Springfield, Illinois,
July 6, 1852 [CW2]

❖

Mr. Clay's eloquence did not consist, as many fine specimens of eloquence do, of types and figures—of antithesis and elegant arrangement
of words and sentences; but rather of that deeply earnest and impassioned
tone and manner, which can proceed only from great sincerity and thorough conviction in the speaker of the justice and importance of his
cause.

—Eulogy on Henry Clay, the State House, Springfield, Illinois,
July 6, 1852 [HSW]

Stephen Douglas

Douglas is a great man—at keeping from answering questions he don't
want to answer.

—Speech, Kalamazoo, Michigan, August 27, 1856 [CW2]

❖

With *me*, the race of ambition has been a failure—a flat failure; with *him*
it has been one of splendid success. His name fills the nation, and is not
unknown even in foreign lands.

—Note on Stephen Douglas, c. December 1856 [CW2]

❖

His tactics just now, in part, is to make it appear that he is having a triumphal entry into and march through the country; but it is all as bom-

bastic and hollow as Napoleon's bulletins sent back from his campaign in Russia.

—Letter to Gustave Koerner, on Stephen Douglas, July 15, 1858 [CW2]

❖

Senator Douglas is of worldwide renown. All the anxious politicians of his party, or who have been of his party for years past, have been looking upon him as certainly, at no distant day, to be the President of the United States. They have seen in his round, jolly, fruitful face post offices, land offices, marshal-ships, and cabinet appointments, charge-ships and foreign missions, bursting and sprouting out in wonderful exuberance ready to be laid hold of by their greedy hands. And as they have been gazing upon this attractive picture so long, they cannot, in the little distraction that has taken place in the party, bring themselves to give up the charming hope; but with greedier anxiety they rush about him, sustain him, and give him marches, triumphal entries, and receptions beyond what even in the days of his highest prosperity they could have brought about in his favor. On the contrary, nobody has ever expected me to be President. In my poor, lean, lank face, nobody has ever seen that any cabbages were sprouting out.

—Speech, Springfield, Illinois, July 17, 1858 [CW2]

❖

I am informed that my distinguished friend yesterday became a little excited, nervous, perhaps, and he said something about *fighting*, as though referring to a pugilistic encounter between him and myself. Did anybody in this audience hear him use such language? I am informed, further, that somebody in *his* audience, rather more excited, or nervous, than himself, took off his coat and offered to take the job off Judge Douglas's hands and fight Lincoln himself. Did anybody here witness that warlike proceeding? Well, I merely desire to say that I shall fight neither Judge Douglas nor his second. I shall not do this for two reasons, which I will now explain. In the first place, a fight would *prove* nothing which is in issue in this contest. It might establish that Judge Douglas is a more muscular man than myself, or it might demonstrate that I am a more muscular man than Judge Douglas. But this question is not referred to in the Cincinnati platform, nor in either of the Springfield platforms. Neither result would prove him right or me wrong. And so of the gentleman who volunteered to do his fighting for him. If my fighting Judge Douglas would not prove anything, it would certainly prove nothing for me to fight his bottle-holder.

—Speech, Havana, Illinois, August 14, 1858 [CW2]

. . . I cannot shake Judge Douglas's teeth loose from the Dred Scott decision. Like some obstinate animal (I mean no disrespect) that will hang
on when he has once got his teeth fixed, you may cut off a leg, or you
may tear away an arm, still he will not relax his hold. And so I may point
out to the Judge and say that he is bespattered all over, from the beginning of his political life to the present time, with attacks upon judicial
decisions—I may cut off limb after limb of his public record, and strive
to wrench him from a single dictum of the Court—yet I cannot divert
him from it. He hangs to the last to the Dred Scott decision.
— First debate with Stephen Douglas, Ottawa, Illinois, August 21, 1858 [CW3]

❖

It is impossible to get the advantage of him. Even if he is worsted, he so
bears himself that the people are bewildered and uncertain as to who has
the better of it.
— Remark on the debating skills of Stephen Douglas
to William Dickson (no date) [RW]

❖

The Judge has set about seriously trying to make the impression that
when we meet at different places I am literally in his clutches—that I am
a poor, helpless, decrepit mouse, and that I can do nothing at all. This is
one of the ways he has taken to create that impression. I don't know any
other way to meet it, except this. I don't want to quarrel with him—to
call him a liar—but when I come square up to him I don't know what
else to call him, if I must tell the truth out.
— Third debate with Stephen Douglas, Jonesboro, Illinois,
September 15, 1858 [CW3]

❖

Trumbull says it was not in the bill when it went to the committee.
When it came back it was in, and Judge Douglas said the alterations were
made by him in combination with Toombs. Trumbull alleges therefore
as his conclusion that Judge Douglas put it in. Then if Douglas wants to
contradict Trumbull and call him a liar, let him say he did not put it in,
and not that he didn't take it out again. It is said that a bear is sometimes
hard enough pushed to drop a cub, and so I presume it was in this case.
I presume the truth is that Douglas put it in and afterwards took it out.
— Fourth debate with Stephen Douglas, on the Toombs Bill,
Charleston, Illinois, September 18, 1858 [CW3]

You all heard me call upon him to say *which of these pieces of evidence was a forgery?* Does he say what I present as a copy of the bill reported by himself is a forgery? . . . *I would then like to know how it comes about, that when each piece of a story is true, the whole story turns out false.* I take it these people have some sense; they see plainly that Judge Douglas is playing cuttlefish, a small species of fish that has no mode of defending itself when pursued except by throwing out a black fluid, which makes the water so dark the enemy cannot see it and thus it escapes. Ain't the Judge playing the cuttlefish?

—Fourth debate with Stephen Douglas, on the Toombs Bill,
Charleston, Illinois, September 18, 1858 [CW3]

❖

In his numerous speeches now being made in Illinois, Senator Douglas regularly argues against the doctrine of the equality of men; and while he does not draw the conclusion that the superiors ought to enslave the inferiors, he evidently wishes his hearers to draw that conclusion. He shirks the responsibility of pulling the house down, but he digs under it that it may fall of its own weight.

—Note, c. October 1, 1858 [CW3]

❖

Whatever may be the result of this ephemeral contest between Judge Douglas and myself, I see the day rapidly approaching when his pill of sectionalism, which he has been thrusting down the throats of Republicans for years past, will be crowded down his own throat.

—Fifth debate with Stephen Douglas, Galesburg, Illinois,
October 7, 1858 [CW3]

❖

Judge Douglas declares that if any community want slavery they have a right to have it. He can say that logically, if he says that there is no wrong in slavery; but if you admit that there is a wrong in it, he cannot logically say that anybody has a right to do wrong.

—Fifth debate with Stephen Douglas, Galesburg, Illinois,
October 7, 1858 [CW3]

❖

And I do think . . . that Judge Douglas, and whoever like him teaches that the negro has no share, humble though it may be, in the Declaration of Independence, is going back to the era of our liberty and independence, and, so far as in him lies, muzzling the cannon that thunders its annual joyous return; that he is blowing out the moral lights around us when he contends that whoever wants slaves has a right to hold them; that he is penetrating, so far as lies in his power, the human soul, and eradicating the light of reason and the love of liberty when he is in every possible way preparing the public mind, by his vast influence, for making the institution of slavery perpetual and national.

—Fifth debate with Stephen Douglas, Galesburg, Illinois,
October 7, 1858 [CW3]

❖

Judge Douglas asks you, "Why cannot the institution of slavery, or rather, why cannot the nation, part slave and part free, continue as our fathers made it *forever?*" In the first place, I insist that our fathers *did not* make this nation half slave and half free, or part slave and part free. I insist that they found the institution of slavery existing here. They did not make it so, but they left it so because they knew of no way to get rid of it at that time. When Judge Douglas undertakes to say that as a matter of choice the fathers of the government made this nation part slave and part free, *he assumes what is historically a falsehood.*

—Sixth debate with Stephen Douglas, Quincy, Illinois,
October 13, 1858 [CW3]

❖

The fight must go on. The cause of civil liberty must not be surrendered at the end of one or even one hundred defeats. Douglas had the ingenuity to be supported in the late contest both as the best means to break down, and to uphold the slave interest. No ingenuity can keep those antagonistic elements in harmony long. Another explosion will soon come.

—Letter to Henry Asbury, after the election of Douglas,
November 19, 1858 [CW3]

❖

I am glad I made the late race. It gave me a hearing on the great and durable question of the age, which I could have had in no other way; and though I now sink out of view, and shall be forgotten, I believe I have made some marks which will tell for the cause of civil liberty long after I am gone.

—Letter to Anson Henry, November 19, 1858 [CW3]

❖

Another "blow-up" is coming; and we shall have fun again. Douglas managed to be supported both as the best instrument to put down and to uphold the slave power; but no ingenuity can long keep these antagonisms in harmony.

—Letter to Charles Ray, November 20, 1858 [CW3]

I expect the result of the election went hard with you. So it did with me, too, perhaps not quite so hard as you may have supposed. I have an abiding faith that we shall beat them in the long run. Step by step the objects of the leaders will become too plain for the people to stand them. I write merely to let you know that I am neither dead nor dying.

—Letter to Alexander Sympson, December 12, 1858 [CW3]

❖

He never lets the logic of principle displace the logic of success.

—Note for a speech on Stephen Douglas, c. September 1859 [CW3]

❖

Douglas's position leads to the nationalization of slavery as surely as does that of Jeff Davis [of Mississippi, future president of the Confederacy] and [James] Mason of Virginia. The two positions are but slightly different roads to the same place—with this difference, that the nationalization of slavery can be reached by Douglas's route, and never can by the other.

—Notes for his speeches at Columbus and Cincinnati, Ohio, September 16–17, 1859 [CW3]

❖

I understand that he [Douglas] has never said, as an individual, whether he thought slavery right or wrong—and he is the only man in the nation that has not! Now such a policy may have a temporary run; it may spring up as necessary to the political prospects of some gentleman; but it is utterly baseless; the people are not indifferent; and it can therefore have no durability or permanence.

—Speech, New Haven, Connecticut, March 6, 1860 [CW4]

Zachary Taylor

General Taylor's battles were not distinguished for brilliant military maneuvers; but in all, he seems rather to have conquered by the exercise of a sober and steady judgment, coupled with a dogged incapacity to understand that defeat was possible. His rarest military trait was a combination of negatives—absence of *excitement* and absence of *fear*. He could not be *flurried*, and he could not be *scared*.

—Eulogy on Zachary Taylor, Chicago, July 24, 1850 [CW2]

❖

The Presidency, even to the most experienced politicians, is no bed of roses; and General Taylor, like others, found thorns within it. No human being can fill that station and escape censure. Still I hope and believe when General Taylor's official conduct shall come to be viewed in the calm light of history, he will be found to have *deserved* as little as any who have succeeded him.

—Eulogy on Zachary Taylor, Chicago, July 24, 1850 [CW2]

❖

. . . the American people, in electing General Taylor to the Presidency, thereby showing their high appreciation of his sterling but unobtrusive qualities, did their *country* a service, and *themselves* an imperishable honor. It is for the young to know that treading the hard path of duty, as he trod it, *will* be noticed, and *will* lead to high places.

—Eulogy on Zachary Taylor, Chicago, July 24, 1850 [CW2]

THE PRESIDENCY

...I must in candor say I do not think myself fit for the presidency. I certainly am flattered and gratified that some partial friends think of me in that connection; but I really think it best for our cause that no concerted effort, such as you suggest, should be made.

—Letter to T. J. Pickett, April 16, 1859 [HSW]

❖

If the rotten democracy shall be beaten in 1860, it has to be done by the North; no human invention can deprive them of the South. I do not deny that there are as good men in the South as the North; and I guess we will elect one of them if he will allow us to do so on Republican ground.

—Letter to Nathan Sargent, June 23, 1859 [CW3]

❖

For my single self, I have enlisted for the permanent success of the Republican cause; and, for this object, I shall labor faithfully in the ranks, unless, as I think not probable, the judgment of the party shall assign me a different position.

—Letter to William Frazer, November 1, 1859 [CW3]

❖

Now, look here, Mr. Bowen, I am not going to make a failure at the Cooper Institute to-morrow night, if I can possibly help it. I am anxious to make a success of it on account of the young men who have so kindly invited me here. It is on my mind all the time, and I cannot be persuaded to accept your hospitality at this time. Please excuse me and let me go to my room at the hotel, lock the door, and there think about my lecture.

—Remark to Henry Bowen, on the Cooper Union Institute speech that led to his Republican party nomination for president, February 26, 1860 [LCU]

❖

Let us have faith that right makes might, and in that faith, let us, to the end, dare to do our duty as we understand it.

—Speech, Cooper Union Institute, New York City, February 27, 1860 [GS]

The speech at New York, being within my calculation before I started, went off passably well, and gave me no trouble whatever. The difficulty was to make nine others before reading audiences who have already seen all my ideas in print.

—Letter to his wife Mary, from Exeter, New Hampshire,
March 4, 1860 [LCU]

❖

My name is new in the field; and I suppose I am not the *first* choice of a very great many. Our policy, then, is to give no offence to others—leave them in a mood to come to us, if they shall be compelled to give up their first love.

—Letter to Samuel Galloway, March 24, 1860 [CW4]

❖

As you request, I will be entirely frank. The taste *is* in my mouth a little; and this, no doubt, disqualifies me, to some extent, to form correct opinions. You may confidently rely, however, that by no advice or consent of mind shall my pretensions be pressed to the point of endangering our common cause.

—Letter to Senator Lyman Trumbull, April 29, 1860 [CW4]

❖

Gentlemen, you had better come up and shake my hand while you can— honors elevate some men.

—Remark to his friends, on receiving news of the Republican
nomination for President, May 18, 1860 [DHD]

❖

Imploring the assistance of Divine Providence, and with due regard to the views and feelings of all who were represented in the Convention; to the rights of all the states, and territories, and people of the nation; to the inviolability of the Constitution, and the perpetual union, harmony, and prosperity of all, I am most happy to cooperate for the practical success of the principles declared by the Convention.

—Letter accepting the presidential nomination, to George Ashmun,
President of the Republican National Convention, May 23, 1860 [HSW]

❖

. . . for personal considerations I would rather have a full term in the Senate—a place in which I would feel more consciously able to discharge the duties required, and where there is more chance to make a reputation, and less danger of losing it—than four years of the presidency.

—Remark to a New York visitor, October 25, 1860 [DHD]

I thank you, in common with all others, who have thought fit, by their votes, to endorse the Republican cause. I rejoice with you in the success which has, so far, attended that cause. Yet in all our rejoicing let us neither express, nor cherish, any harsh feeling towards any citizen who, by his vote, has differed with us. Let us at all times remember that all American citizens are brothers of a common country, and should dwell together in the bonds of fraternal feeling.

—Remarks to "friends and fellow-citizens," Springfield, Illinois, November 20, 1860 [CW4]

❖

It seems to me that Douglas got the best of it at the election last fall. I am left to face an empty treasury and a great rebellion, while my own party endorses his popular sovereignty idea and applies it in legislation. . . . I only wish I could have got there to lock the door before the horse was stolen. But when I get to the spot, I can find the tracks.

—Remarks to his friend Joseph Gillespie, as he left for Washington, D.C., February 11, 1861 [RW]

❖

I, as already intimated, am but an accidental instrument, temporary, and to serve but for a limited time, but I appeal to you again to constantly bear in mind that with you, and not with politicians, not with Presidents, not with office-seekers, but with you, is the question, "Shall the Union and shall the liberties of this country be preserved to the latest generation?"

—Speech, from the platform of his train, to Governor Oliver Morton and the citizens of Indiana, February 11, 1861 [CW4]

❖

I have been selected to fill an important office for a brief period, and am now, in your eyes, invested with an influence which will soon pass away; but should my administration prove to be a very wicked one, or what is more probable, a very foolish one, if you, the people, are but true to yourselves and to the Constitution, there is but little harm I can do, *thank God!*

—Speech to his "fellow-countrymen," Lawrenceburg, Indiana, February 12, 1861 [CW4]

❖

There was a man who was to be nominated at a political convention and hired a horse of a livery keeper to journey there. The horse was so confoundedly slow, however, that the man arrived too late, and found his opponent nominated and the convention adjourned. When he arrived home he said to the stableman, "This is a fine animal of yours—a fine animal." "Do you think so?" "Certainly, but never sell him to an undertaker." "Undertaker! Why not?" "Because if the horse were hitched to a hearse, resurrection day would come before he reached the cemetery." So if my journey goes on at this slow rate it will be resurrection day before I reach the capital.

—Anecdote recounted to a crowd at a station stop on his train to
Washington, D.C., February 1861 [RW]

❖

It is true that while I hold myself without mock modesty the humblest of all individuals that have ever been elevated to the Presidency, I have a more difficult task to perform than any one of them.

—Speech to the New York State Legislature, Albany, New York,
February 18, 1861 [CW4]

❖

I shall endeavor to take the ground I deem most just to the North, the East, the West, the South, and the whole country. I take it, I hope, in good temper—certainly with no malice toward any section. I shall do all that may be in my power to promote a peaceful settlement of all our difficulties. The man does not live who is more devoted to peace than I am. None who would do more to preserve it. But it may be necessary to put the foot down firmly. And if I do my duty, and do right, you will sustain me, will you not?

—Speech to the New Jersey State Assembly, February 21, 1861 [HSW]

❖

It shall be my endeavor to preserve the peace of this country so far as it can possibly be done, consistently with the maintenance of the institutions of the country. With my consent, or without my great displeasure, this country shall never witness the shedding of one drop of blood in fraternal strife.

—Speech to Governor Andrew Curtin and the citizens of
Pennsylvania, Harrisburg, Pennsylvania, February 22, 1861 [CW4]

❖

While the people retain their virtue and vigilance, no administration, by any extreme of wickedness or folly, can very seriously injure the government in the short space of four years.

—First inaugural address, March 4, 1861 [CWBQ]

If I were to try to read, much less answer, all the attacks made on me, this shop might as well be closed for any other business. I do the very best I know how—the very best I can; and I mean to keep doing so until the end. If the end brings me out all right, what is said against me won't amount to anything. If the end brings me out wrong, ten thousand angels swearing I was right would make no difference.

> —Remark to an officer suggesting the President refute
> "an attack made on him by the Congressional Committee
> on the Conduct of the War" (no date) [YS]

❖

If there be those who would not save the Union unless they could at the same time destroy slavery, I do not agree with them. My paramount object in this struggle is to save the Union, and is not either to save or destroy slavery. If I could save the Union without freeing any slave, I would do it; and if I could save it by freeing all the slaves, I would do it; and if I could save it by freeing some and leaving others alone, I would also do that. What I do about slavery and the colored race, I do because I believe it helps to save the Union; and what I forbear, I forbear because I do not believe it would help to save the Union.

> —"Executive Mansion" reply to Horace Greeley's *New York Tribune*
> editorial "The Prayer of Twenty Millions," August 22, 1862 [CWBQ]

❖

With all the fearful strain that is upon me night and day, if I did not laugh I should die.

> —Remark to a cabinet minister who wondered why Lincoln
> was reading a book of humor [LAIKH]

❖

Well, I would be very happy to oblige you, if my passes were respected; but the fact is, sir, that I have within the last two years given passes to two hundred and fifty thousand men to go to Richmond, and not one has got there yet.

> —Remark to "a gentleman" who had "solicited a pass
> for Richmond," (no date) [ALL]

❖

As a pilot, I have used my best exertions to keep afloat our ship of State, and shall be glad to resign my trust at the appointed time to another pilot more skillful and successful than I may prove. In every case, and at all hazards, the Government must be perpetuated. Relying, as I do, upon the Almighty Power, and encouraged as I am by these resolutions which you

have just read, with the support which I receive from Christian men, I
shall not hesitate to use all the means at my control to secure the termination of this rebellion, and will hope for success.
—Reply to a committee from the Presbyterian General Assembly,
June 2, 1863 [CW6]

❖

I have here some papers which I started in this morning to carefully examine. They contain the entire proceedings of a military court for the trial of
a young soldier for desertion. And they contain minutes of the testimony
taken on the trial, together with the conviction and sentence to death of the
boy, I have read just three pages of the testimony, and have found this: "The
boy said when first arrested that he was going home to see his mother." I
don't think that I can allow a boy to be shot who tried to go home to see
his mother. I guess I don't want to read any more of this.
—Remark to Minnesota Senator Morton Smith Wilkinson,
summer 1863 [RW]

❖

Well, I've got something now that I can give to everybody.
—Remark after catching varioloid, a contagious disease,
c. December 1863 [ALL]

❖

It is my conviction that, had the Proclamation been issued even six
months earlier than it was, public sentiment would not have sustained it.
Just so as to the subsequent action in reference to enlisting blacks in the
border states. The step, taken sooner, could not, in my judgment, have
been carried out. A man watches his pear tree day after day, impatient for
the ripening of the fruit. Let him attempt to force the process, and he
may spoil both fruit and tree. But let him patiently wait, and the ripe pear
at length falls into his lap. We have seen this great revolution in public
sentiment slowly but surely progressing, so that, when final action came,
the opposition was not strong enough to defeat the purpose.
—Remark to his portrait painter Francis Carpenter, 1864 [RW]

❖

Some of my generals complain that I impair discipline and subordination
in the army by my pardons and respites, but it makes me rested after a
day's hard work if I can find some good excuse for saving a man's life,
and I go to bed happy as I think how joyous the signing of my name will
make him and his family and friends.
—Remark to Schuyler Colfax, Speaker of the House of Representatives,
c. 1864 [RW]

Oh, dear, dear! These cases kill me! I wish I didn't have to hear about them! What shall I do? You make the laws, and then you come with heartbroken women and ask me to set them aside. You have decided that if a soldier raises his hand against his superior officer, as this man has done, he shall die! Then if I leave the laws to be executed, one of these distressing scenes occurs, which almost kills me.

> —Remark to Congressmen who had just witnessed a woman's appeal for a commutation of her husband's death sentence (no date) [RW]

❖

To remove a man is very easy, but when I go to fill his place, there are twenty applicants, and of these I must make nineteen enemies.

> —Remark to his portrait painter Francis Carpenter, c. 1864 [DHD]

❖

The fact is . . . I have got more pigs than I have teats.

> —Remark on political patronage to Congressman Luther Hanchett (no date) [RW]

❖

He is like Jim Jett's brother. Jim used to say that his brother was the damndest scoundrel that ever lived, but in the infinite mercy of Providence he was also the damndest fool.

> —Remark to his secretary John Hay, on the rumor that General John C. Fremont would run against him for the Republican nomination for President, May 22, 1864 [ALL]

❖

This is the third time he has thrown this at me, and I do not think I am called on to continue to beg him to take it back, especially when the country would not go to destruction in consequence. . . . On the whole, Brough, I reckon you had better let it alone this time.

> —Remark to Ohio Governor John Brough, on Secretary of the Treasury Salmon Chase's offered resignation, June 1864 [DHD]

❖

Your resignation of the office of Secretary of the Treasury, sent me yesterday, is accepted. Of all I have said in commendation of your ability and fidelity, I have nothing to unsay; and yet you and I have reached a point of mutual embarrassment in our official relation which it seems cannot be overcome, or longer sustained, consistently with the public service.

> —Letter to Salmon Chase, June 30, 1864 [CW7]

I happen temporarily to occupy this big White House. I am a living witness what any one of your children may look to come here as my father's child has. It is in order that each of you may have through this free government which we have enjoyed an open field and a fair chance for your industry, enterprise and intelligence; that you may all have equal privileges in the race of life, with all its desirable human aspirations. It is for this the struggle should be maintained, that we may not lose our birthright—not only for one, but for two or three years. The nation is worth fighting for to secure such an inestimable jewel.

—Speech to 166th Ohio Regiment, August 22, 1864 [CW7]

❖

This morning, as for some days past, it seems exceedingly probable that this Administration will not be reelected. Then it will be my duty to so cooperate with the President-elect as to save the Union between the election and the inauguration; as he will have secured his election on such ground that he cannot possibly save it afterwards.

—Memorandum, August 23, 1864 [CWBQ]

❖

You think I don't know I am going to be beaten, *but I do*, and unless some great change takes place, *badly beaten*.

—Remark on the coming presidential election, August 1864.
(This "great change" took place, most notably with General William Tecumseh Sherman's taking of Atlanta in early September.) [DHD]

❖

I confess that I desire to be re-elected. God knows I do not want the labor and responsibility of the office for another four years. But I have the common pride of humanity to wish my past four years Administration endorsed.

—Remark, c. 1864 [DHD]

❖

I am struggling to maintain government, not to overthrow it. I am struggling especially to prevent others from overthrowing it. I therefore say, that if I shall live, I shall remain President until the fourth of next March; and that whoever shall be constitutionally elected therefore in November shall be duly installed as President on the fourth of March; and that in the interval I shall do my utmost that whoever is to hold the helm for the next voyage shall start with the best possible chance to save the ship.

—Response to a serenade by a group of Maryland citizens,
October 19, 1864 [CW8]

It does look as if the people wanted me to stay here a little longer, and I suppose I shall have to, if they do.
  —Remark overheard by the diarist George Templeton Strong, 1864 [DHD]

❖

Being only mortal, after all, I should have been a little mortified if I had been beaten in this canvas before the people; but that sting would have been more than compensated by the thought that the people had notified me that all my official responsibilities were soon to be lifted off my back.
  —Remark to Noah Brooks, November 9, 1864 [RW]

❖

We cannot have free government without elections; and if the rebellion could force us to forego, or postpone, a national election, it might fairly claim to have already conquered and ruined us.
  —Address to a congratulatory serenade on his reelection,
November 10, 1864 [HSW]

❖

Human nature will not change. In any future great national trial, compared with the men of this, we shall have as weak and as strong; as silly and as wise; as bad and as good. Let us therefore study the incidents of this, as philosophy to learn wisdom from, and none of them as wrongs to be revenged.
  —Address to a congratulatory serenade on his reelection,
November 10, 1864 [HSW]

❖

. . . now that the election is over, may not all, having a common interest, reunite in a common effort, to save our common country?
  —Address to a congratulatory serenade on his reelection,
November 10, 1864 [CW8]

❖

Having served four years in the depths of a great, and yet unended national peril, I can view this call to a second term, in nowise more flatteringly to myself, than as an expression of the public judgment that I may better finish a difficult work in which I have labored from the first, than could anyone less severely schooled to the task.
  —Reply to Representative James Wilson of Iowa, Senator Lyman Trumbull
and Representative John Dawson of Pennsylvania, who comprised
a committee that officially informed him of his second election as President,
March 1, 1865 [CW8]

RELIGION, MORALITY, AND HUMAN FRAILTY

The *preacher*, it is said, advocates temperance because he is a fanatic, and desires a union of the Church and State; the *lawyer*, from his pride and vanity of hearing himself speak; and the *hired agent*, for his salary. But when one who has long been known as a victim of intemperance bursts the fetters that have bound him, and appears before his neighbors "clothed, and in his right mind," a redeemed specimen of long lost humanity, and stands up with tears of joy trembling in eyes to tell of the miseries *once* endured, *now* to be endured no more forever; of his once naked and starving children now clad and fed comfortably; of a wife long weighed down with woe, weeping, and a broken heart, now restored to health, happiness and renewed affection; and how easily it all is done, once it is resolved to be done; however simple his language, there is a logic, and an eloquence in it, that few, with human feelings, can resist. They cannot say that *he* desires a union of church and state, for he is not a church member; they cannot say *he* is vain of hearing himself speak, for his whole demeanor shows he would gladly avoid speaking at all; they cannot say *he* speaks for pay for he receives none, and asks for none. Nor can his sincerity in any way be doubted, or his sympathy for those he would persuade to imitate his example be denied.

> —Speech to the Springfield Washington Temperance Society,
> February 22, 1842 [HSW]

❖

When the dram-seller and drinker were incessantly told, not in the accents of entreaty and persuasion, diffidently addressed by erring man to an erring brother, but in the thundering tones of anathema and denunciation with which the lordly Judge often groups together all the crimes of the felon's life and thrusts them in his face just ere he passes sentence of death upon him that *they* were the authors of all the vice and misery and crime in the land; that *they* were the manufacturers and material of all the thieves and robbers and murderers that infested the earth; that *their* houses were the workshops of the devil; and that *their persons* should be shunned by all the good and virtuous as moral pestilences—I say, when they were told all this, and in this way, it is not wonderful that they were slow, very slow, to acknowledge the truth of such denunciations, and to join the ranks of their denouncers in a hue and cry against themselves.

—Speech to the Springfield Washington Temperance Society,
February 22, 1842 [HSW]

❖

When the conduct of men is designed to be influenced, *persuasion*, kind, unassuming persuasion, should ever be adopted.

—Speech to the Springfield Washington Temperance Society,
February 22, 1842 [HSW]

❖

In my judgment, such of us as have never fallen victims have been spared more from the absence of appetite than from any mental or moral superiority over those who have.

—Speech to the Springfield Washington Temperance Society,
February 22, 1842 [HSW]

❖

That I am not a member of any Christian church is true; but I have never denied the truth of the Scriptures; and I have never spoken with intentional disrespect of religion in general, or of any denomination of Christians in particular.

. . . I do not think I could myself be brought to support a man for office whom I knew to be an open enemy of, and scoffer at, religion.

—To the voters of the Seventh Congressional District on the charge
that he was an "open scoffer" at religion, July 31, 1846 [CW1]

❖

I believe it is an established maxim in morals that he who makes an assertion without knowing whether it is true or false is guilty of falsehood; and the accidental truth of the assertion does not justify or excuse him.

—Letter to the editor, *Illinois Gazette,* August 11, 1846 [HSW]

❖

Pharaoh's country was cursed with plagues, and his hosts were drowned in the Red Sea for striving to retain a captive people who had already served them more than four hundred years. May like disasters never befall us!

—Eulogy on Henry Clay, the State House, Springfield, Illinois,
July 6, 1852 [HSW]

❖

I have noticed in Southern newspapers, particularly the Richmond *Enquirer*, the Southern view of the Free States. They insist that slavery has a right to spread. They defend it upon principle. They insist that their slaves are far better off than Northern freemen. What a mistaken view do these men have of Northern laborers! They think that men are always to remain laborers here—but there is no such class. The men who labored for another last year, this year labors for himself, and next year he will hire others to labor for him. These men don't understand when they think in this manner of Northern free labor.

—Speech, Kalamazoo, Michigan, August 27, 1856 [CW2]

❖

Free labor has the inspiration of hope; pure slavery has no hope. The power of hope upon human exertion and happiness is wonderful.

—Note on labor, c. September 17, 1859 [CW3]

❖

Constituted as man is, he has positive need of occasional recreation, and whatever can give him this, associated with virtue and advantage and free from vice and disadvantage, is a positive good.

—Speech to the Wisconsin State Agricultural Society,
Milwaukee, Wisconsin, September 30, 1859 [HSW]

❖

Free labor argues that as the Author of man makes every individual with one head and one pair of hands, it was probably intended that heads and hands should cooperate as friends, and that that particular head should direct and control that particular pair of hands. As each man has one mouth to be fed and one pair of hands to furnish food, it was probably intended that that particular pair of hands should feed that particular mouth—that each head is the natural guardian, director and protector of the hands and mouth inseparably connected with it; and that being so, every head should be cultivated and improved by whatever will add to its capacity for performing its charge. In one word, free labor insists on universal education.

—Speech to the Wisconsin State Agricultural Society,
Milwaukee, Wisconsin, September 30, 1859 [HSW]

It is said an Eastern monarch once charged his wise men to invent him a sentiment to be ever in view, and which should be true and appropriate in all times and situations. They presented him the words, "*And this, too, shall pass away.*" How much it expresses! How chastening in the hour of pride; how consoling in the depths of affliction! "And this, too, shall pass away." And yet, let us hope it is not *quite* true. Let us hope, rather, that by the best cultivation of the physical world, beneath and around us, and the intellectual and moral worlds within us, we shall secure an individual, social, and political prosperity and happiness whose course shall be onward and upward, and which, while the earth endures, shall not pass away.

—Speech to the Wisconsin State Agricultural Society,
Milwaukee, Wisconsin, September 30, 1859 [HSW]

❖

When one starts poor, as most do in the race of life, free society is such that he knows he can better his condition; he knows that there is no fixed condition of labor for his whole life. I am not ashamed to confess that twenty-five years ago I was a hired laborer, mauling rails, at work on a flatboat—just what might happen to any poor man's son! I want every man to have the chance—and I believe a black man is entitled to it—in which he *can* better his condition—when he may look forward and hope to be a hired laborer this year and the next, work for himself afterward, and finally to hire men to work for him.

—Speech, New Haven, Connecticut, March 6, 1860 [CW4]

❖

Here are twenty-three ministers of different denominations, and all of them are against me but three; and here are a great many prominent members of the churches, a very large majority of whom are against me. Mr. Bateman, I am not a Christian—God knows I would be one, but I have carefully read the Bible, and I do not so understand this book [drawing forth a pocket New Testament]. These men well know that I am for freedom in the territories, freedom everywhere as far as the Constitution and laws will permit, and that my opponents are for slavery. They know this and yet, with this book in their hands, in the light of which human bondage cannot live a moment, they are going to vote against me. I do not understand it at all.

—Remark to Illinois superintendent of public instruction
Newton Bateman, late October 1860 [RW]

The fact is, I don't like to hear cut and dried sermons. No—when I hear a man preach, I like to see him act as if he were fighting bees!
—Remark to the sculptor Leonard Wells Volk, c. 1860 [LAIKH]

❖

Since your last annual assembling another year of health and bountiful harvests has passed. And while it has not pleased the Almighty to bless us with a return of peace, we can but press on, guided by the best light He gives us, trusting that in His own good time and wise way all will yet be well.
—Annual Message to Congress, December 1, 1862 [GS]

❖

It is most cheering and encouraging for me to know that in the efforts which I have made and am making for the restoration of a righteous peace to our country, I am upheld and sustained by the good wishes and prayers of God's people. No one is more deeply than myself aware that without His favor our highest wisdom is but as foolishness and that our most strenuous efforts would avail nothing in the shadow of His displeasure. I am conscious of no desire for my country's welfare that is not in consonance with His will, and of no plan upon which we may not ask His blessing. It seems to me that if there be one subject upon which all good men may unitedly agree, it is imploring the gracious favor of the God of Nations upon the struggles our people are making for the preservation of their precious birthright of civil and religious liberty.
—Letter to Caleb Russell and Sallie Fenton of the Religious Society of Friends, Iowa, January 5, 1863 [CW6]

❖

I have often wished that I was a more devout man than I am.
—Remarks to the Presbyterian Synod of Baltimore, October 24, 1863 [CW6]

❖

On principle I dislike an oath which requires a man to swear he *has* not done wrong. It rejects the Christian principle of forgiveness on terms of repentance. I think it is enough if the man does no wrong *hereafter*.
—Letter to Secretary of War Edwin Stanton, February 5, 1864 [CW7]

I claim not to have controlled events, but confess plainly that events have controlled me. . . . If God now wills the removal of a great wrong, and wills also that we of the North as well as you of the South shall pay fairly for our complicity in that wrong, impartial history will find therein new cause to attest and revere the justice and goodness of God.

—Letter to Albert G. Hodges, April 4, 1864 [CW7]

❖

The purposes of the Almighty are perfect, and must prevail, though we erring mortals may fail to accurately perceive them in advance. We hoped for a happy termination of this terrible war long before this, but God knows best, and has ruled otherwise. . . . we must work earnestly in the best light He gives us, trusting that so working still conduces to the great ends He ordains. Surely He intends some great good to follow this mighty convulsion, which no mortal could make, and no mortal could stay.

—Letter to Eliza Gurney, September 4, 1864 [HSW]

❖

When, a year or two ago, those professedly holy men of the South met in the semblance of prayer and devotion, and, in the name of Him who said, "As ye would all men should do unto you, do ye even so unto them," appealed to the Christian world to aid them in doing to a whole race of men as they would have no man do unto themselves, to my thinking, they contemned and insulted God and His church far more than did Satan when he tempted the Savior with the Kingdoms of the earth. The devil's attempt was no more false and far less hypocritical. But let me forbear, remembering it is also written, "Judge not, lest ye be judged."

—Letter to the Reverend George B. Ide, J.R. Doolittle, and A. Hubbell, May 30, 1864 [CW7]

❖

. . . I, Abraham Lincoln, President of the United States, do hereby appoint and set apart the last Thursday in November next as a day which I desire to be observed by all my fellow citizens wherever they may then be as a day of Thanksgiving and Praise to Almighty God the beneficent Creator and Ruler of the Universe. And I do farther recommend to my fellow citizens aforesaid that on that occasion they do reverently humble themselves in the dust and from thence offer up penitent and fervent prayers and supplications to the Great Disposer of events for a turn of the inestimable blessings of Peace, Union and Harmony throughout the

land, which it has pleased him to assign as a dwelling place for ourselves and for our posterity throughout all generations.
—Thanksgiving proclamation, October 20, 1864 [CW8]

❖

You say your husband is a religious man; tell him when you meet him that I say I am not much of a judge of religion, but that, in my opinion, the religion that sets men to rebel and fight against their government, because, as they think, that government does not sufficiently help *some* men to eat their bread on the sweat of *other* men's faces, is not the sort of religion upon which people can get to heaven.
—Remarks to two women from Tennessee asking for the release of their rebel husbands as prisoners of war, December 6, 1864 [CW8]

❖

Fondly do we hope—fervently do we pray—that this mighty scourge of war may speedily pass away. Yet, if God wills that it continue until all the wealth piled by the bondman's two hundred and fifty years of unrequited toil shall be sunk, and until every drop of blood drawn with the lash shall be paid by another drawn with the sword, as was said three thousand years ago, so still it must be said:
The judgments of the Lord are true, and righteous altogether.
—Letter to Amanda Hall, March 20, 1865 [CW8]

SECESSION

We, the majority, would not strive to dissolve the Union; and if any attempt is made it must be you, who so loudly stigmatize us as disunionists. But the Union, in any event, won't be dissolved. We don't want to dissolve it, and if you attempt it, *we won't let you*. With the purse and the sword, the army and navy and treasury in our hands and at our command, you *couldn't do it*. This Government would be very weak, indeed, if a majority, with a disciplined army and navy, and a well-filled treasury, could not preserve itself when attacked by an unarmed, undisciplined, unorganized minority.

All this talk about the dissolution of the Union is humbug—nothing but folly. *We* WON'T dissolve the Union, and *you* SHAN'T.

—Speech, Galena, Illinois, July 23, 1856 [CW2]

❖

. . . you will not abide the election of a Republican President! In that supposed event, you say you will destroy the Union; and then you say the great crime of having destroyed it will be upon us! That is cool. A highwayman holds a pistol to my ear, and mutters through his teeth, "Stand and deliver, or I shall kill you, and then you will be a murderer!"

—Speech, Cooper Union Institute, New York City, February 27, 1860 [LCU]

❖

Let there be no compromise on the question of extending slavery. If there is, all our labor is lost, and, ere long, must be done again. The dangerous ground—that into which some of our friends have a hankering to run—is Popular Sovereignty. Have none of it. Stand firm. The tug has to come, and better now than at any time hereafter.

—Letter to Senator Lyman Trumbull, December 10, 1860 [CWBQ]

❖

Do the people of the South really entertain fears that a Republican administration would, directly or indirectly, interfere with their slaves or with them about their slaves? If they do, I wish to assure you, as once a friend, and still, I hope, not an enemy, that there is no cause for such fears.

—Letter to Alexander Stephens (future vice president of the Confederate States), December 22, 1860 [HSW]

❖

What is our present condition? We have just carried an election on principles fairly stated to the people. Now we are told in advance the government shall be broken up unless we surrender to those we have beaten before we take the offices. In this they are either attempting to play upon us, or they are in dead earnest. Either way, if we surrender, it is the end of us and of the government. They will repeat the experiment upon us *ad libitum*. A year will not pass till we shall have to take Cuba as a condition upon which they will stay in the Union.

—Letter to James Hale, January 11, 1861 [CW4]

❖

I will suffer death before I will consent or will advise my friend to consent to any concession or compromise which looks like buying the privilege to take possession of this government to which we have a constitutional right.

—Remark to a journalist from the *New York Herald*, January 28, 1861 [DHD]

❖

I hold that in contemplation of universal law and of the Constitution, the Union of these States is perpetual. Perpetuity is implied, if not expressed, in the fundamental law of all national governments. It is safe to assert that no government proper ever had a provision in its organic law for its own termination. Continue to execute all the express provisions of our national Constitution, and the Union will endure forever—it being impossible to destroy it, except by some action not provided for in the instrument itself.

—First inaugural address, March 4, 1861 [GS]

❖

That there are persons in one section or another who seek to destroy the Union at all events, and are glad of any pretext to do it, I will neither affirm or deny; but if there be such, I need address no word to them. To those, however, who really love the Union, may I not speak?

Before entering upon so grave a matter as the destruction of our national fabric, with all its benefits, its memories and hopes, would it not be wise to ascertain precisely why we do it? Will you hazard so desperate a step while there is any possibility that any portion of the ills you fly from have no real existence? Will you while the certain ills you fly to are greater than all the real ones you fly from? Will you risk the commission of so fearful a mistake?

—First inaugural address, March 4, 1861 [GS]

❖

Plainly, the central idea of secession is the essence of anarchy. A majority, held in restraint by constitutional checks and limitations and always changing easily with deliberate changes of popular opinions and sentiments, is the only true sovereign of a free people. Whoever rejects it does, of necessity, fly to anarchy or to despotism. Unamimity is impossible; the rule of a minority, as a permanent arrangement, is wholly inadmissible; so that, rejecting the majority principle, anarchy or despotism in some form is all that is left.

—First inaugural address, March 4, 1861 [GS]

❖

If it were admitted that you who are dissatisfied hold the right side in the dispute, there still is no single good reason for precipitate action. Intelligence, patriotism, Christianity, and a firm reliance on Him who has never yet forsaken this favored land are still competent to adjust, in the best way, all our present difficulty.

—First inaugural address, March 4, 1861 [CWBQ]

❖

In *your* hands, my dissatisfied fellow countrymen, and not in *mine*, is the momentous issue of civil war. The government will not assail *you*. You can have no conflict without being yourselves the aggressors. *You* have no oath registered in heaven to destroy the government, while *I* shall have the most solemn one to "preserve, protect and defend" it.

—First inaugural address, March 4, 1861 [GS]

❖

The States have their *status* in the Union, and they have no other *legal status*. If they break from this, they can only do so against law and by revolution. The Union, and not themselves separately, procured their independence and their liberty. By conquest, or purchase, the Union gave each of them whatever of independence and liberty it has.

—Message to Congress in Special Session, July 4, 1861 [GS]

Great honor is due to those officers who remained true, despite the example of their treacherous associates; but the greatest honor, and most
important fact of all, is the unanimous firmness of the common soldiers
and common sailors. To the last man, so far as is known, they have successfully resisted the traitorous efforts of those whose commands, but an
hour before, they obeyed as absolute law. This is the patriotic instinct of
plain people. They understand, without an argument, that the destroying
the Government which was made by Washington means no good to
them.

—Message to Congress in Special Session, July 4, 1861 [GS]

❖

I most cordially sympathize with your Excellency in the wish to preserve
the peace of my own native State, Kentucky; but it is with regret I search,
and cannot find, in your not very short letter, any declaration, or intima-
tion, that you entertain any desire for the preservation of the Federal
Union.

—Letter to Governor of Kentucky Beriah Magoffin, August 24, 1861 [CW4]

❖

I think to lose Kentucky is nearly the same as to lose the whole game.
Kentucky gone, we cannot hold Missouri, nor, as I think, Maryland.
These all against us, and the job on our hands is too large for us. We
would as well consent to separation at once, including the surrender of
this capitol.

—Letter to Orville Browning, September 22, 1861 [CW4]

❖

The right of a State to secede is not an open or debatable question.

—Remark to his secretary John Nicolay, December 13, 1861 [RW]

❖

The division of a State is dreaded as a precedent. But a measure made ex-
pedient by a war is no precedent for times of peace. It is said that the admission of West Virginia is secession, and tolerated only because it is our
secession. Well, if we call it by that name, there is still difference enough
between secession against the Constitution, and secession in favor of the
Constitution.

—Draft opinion on the admission of West Virginia
into the Union, c. December 31, 1862 [CW6]

We all agree that the seceded States, so called, are out of their proper practical relation with the Union; and that the sole object of the government, civil and military, in regard to those States, is to again get them into that proper practical relation. I believe it is not only possible, but in fact easier to do this, without deciding, or even considering, whether these States have ever been out of the Union than with it.

—Last speech, from a White House balcony, April 11, 1865 [HSW]

SLAVERY AND
THE EMANCIPATION PROCLAMATION

You say A. is white, and B. is black. It is *color*, then; the lighter having the right to enslave the darker? Take care. By this rule, you are to be slave to the first man you meet with a fairer skin than your own.

—Notes, c. July 1846 [HSW]

❖

What *natural* right required Kansas and Nebraska to be opened to slavery? Is not slavery universally granted to be, in the abstract, a gross outrage on the law of nature? Have not all civilized nations, our own among them, made the slave trade capital, and classed it with piracy and murder? Is it not held to be the great wrong of the world? Do not the Southern people, the slaveholders themselves, spurn the domestic slave dealer, refuse to associate with him, or let their families associate with his family as long as the taint of his infamous calling is known?

—Speech, Springfield, Illinois, October 4, 1854 [CW2]

❖

. . . let me say that I think I have no prejudice against the Southern people. They are just what we would be in their situation. If slavery did not now exist amongst them, they would not introduce it. If it did now exist amongst us, we should not instantly give it up—this I believe of the masses north and south.

—Speech, Peoria, Illinois, October 16, 1854 [HSW]

❖

Slavery is founded in the selfishness of man's nature—opposition to it is his love of justice.

—Speech, Peoria, Illinois, October 16, 1854 [HSW]

❖

The question of slavery, at the present day, should be not only the greatest question, but very nearly the sole question.

—Speech, Kalamazoo, Michigan, August 27, 1856 [CW2]

❖

You will find that all the arguments in favor of king-craft were of this class; they always bestrode the necks of the people, not that they wanted to do it, but because the people were better off for being ridden. That is their argument, and this argument of the Judge [Stephen Douglas] is the same old serpent that says you work and I eat, you toil and I will enjoy the fruits of it. Turn it whatever way you will—whether it come from the mouth of a King [as] an excuse for enslaving the people of his country, or from the mouth of men of one race as a reason for enslaving the men of another race, it is all the same old serpent, and I hold if that course of argumentation that is made for the purpose of convincing the public mind that we should not care about this should be granted, it does not stop with the negro. I should like to know if taking this old Declaration of Independence, which declares that all men are equal upon principle, and making exceptions to it, where will it stop? If one man says it does not mean a negro, why not another say it does not mean some other man?

—Speech, Chicago, July 10, 1858 [CW2]

❖

I have always hated slavery, I think, as much as any Abolitionist. I have been an Old Line Whig. I have always hated it, but I have always been quiet about it until this new era of the introduction of the Nebraska bill began. I always believed that everybody was against it, and it was in course of ultimate extinction.

—Speech, Chicago, July 10, 1858 [HSW]

❖

I have said I do not understand the Declaration to mean that all men were created equal in all respects. They are not our equal in color; but I suppose that it does mean to declare that all men are equal in some respects; they are equal in their right to "life, liberty and the pursuit of happiness." . . . All I ask for the negro is that if you do not like him, let him alone.

—Speech, Chicago, July 10, 1858 [HSW]

❖

Slavery is not a matter of little importance: it overshadows every other question in which we are interested. It has divided the Methodist and

Presbyterian churches, and has sown discord in the American Tract Society. The churches have split, and the Society will follow their example before long. So it will be seen that slavery is agitated in the religious as well as in the political world.

—Speech, Clinton, Illinois, September 2, 1858 [CW3]

❖

Suppose it is true that the negro is inferior to the white in the gifts of nature; is it not the exact reverse justice that the white should, for that reason, take from the negro any part of the little which has been given him? "*Give* to him that is needy" is the Christian rule of charity; but "Take from him that is needy" is the rule of slavery.

—Note, c. October 1, 1858 [HSW]

❖

As a good thing, slavery is strikingly peculiar, in this, that it is the only good thing which no man ever seeks the good of *for himself*!

Nonsense! Wolves devouring lambs, not because it is good for their own greedy maws, but because it is good for the lambs!

—Note, c. October 1, 1858 [CW3]

❖

... we know from Judge Douglas himself that slavery began to be an element of discord among the white people of this country as far back as 1699, or one hundred and sixty years ago, or five generations of men—counting thirty years to a generation. Now it would seem to me that it might have occurred to Judge Douglas, or anybody who had turned his attention to these facts, that there was something in the nature of that thing, slavery, somewhat durable for mischief and discord.

—Speech, Columbus, Ohio, September 16, 1859 [CW3]

❖

He [Thomas Jefferson] supposed there was a question of God's eternal justice wrapped up in the enslaving of any race of men, or any man, and that those who did so braved the arm of Jehovah—that when a nation thus dared the Almighty every friend of that nation had cause to dread His wrath. Choose ye between Jefferson and Douglas as to what is the true view of this element among us.

—Speech, Columbus, Ohio, September 16, 1859 [CW3]

One section of our country believes slavery is *right*, and ought to be extended, while the other believes it is *wrong*, and ought not to be extended. This is the only substantial dispute.

—First Inaugural Address, March 4, 1861 [GS]

❖

We must free the slaves or be ourselves subdued. The slaves were undeniably an element of strength to those who had their service, and we must decide whether that element should be with us or against us.

—Remark to Secretary of the Navy Gideon Welles, July 13, 1862.
(On July 22, Lincoln broached to his cabinet his intention
to issue an emancipation proclamation.) [CWBQ]

❖

Would my word free the slaves, when I cannot even enforce the Constitution in the rebel states?

—Remark to a group of ministers from Chicago,
September 13, 1862 [CWBQ]

❖

What good would a proclamation of emancipation from me do, especially as we are now situated? I do not want to issue a document that the whole world will see must necessarily be inoperative, like the Pope's bull against the comet!

—Remark to a group of ministers from Chicago, September 13, 1862 [CW5]

❖

It is my earnest desire to know the will of Providence in this matter [of emancipation]. *And if I can learn what it is I will do it!*

—Remark to a group of ministers from Chicago, September 13, 1862 [CW5]

❖

When the rebel army was at Frederick, I determined, as soon as it should be driven out of Maryland, to issue a proclamation of emancipation, such as I thought most likely to be useful. I said nothing to anyone; but I made the promise to myself and to my Maker. The rebel army is now driven out, and I am going to fulfill that promise.

—Remark to his cabinet, September 22, 1862 [CWBQ]

❖

. . . on the first day of January in the year of our Lord, one thousand eight hundred and sixty-three, all persons held as slaves within any state, or des-

ignated part of a state, the people whereof shall then be in rebellion against the United States shall be then, thenceforward, and forever free . . .
—Preliminary Emancipation Proclamation, September 22, 1862 [CWBQ]

❖

Without slavery the rebellion could never have existed; without slavery it could not continue.
—Annual Message to Congress, December 1, 1862 [GS]

❖

In giving freedom to the *slave*, we *assure* freedom to the *free*—honorable alike in what we give, and what we preserve. We shall nobly save, or meanly lose, the last best hope of earth.
—Annual Message to Congress, December 1, 1862 [GS]

❖

I never in my life felt more certain that I was doing right than I do in signing this paper. But I have been receiving calls and shaking hands since nine o'clock this morning till my arm is stiff and numb. Now, this signature is one that will be closely examined, and if they find my hand trembled, they will say, "He had some compunctions." But, anyway, it is going to be done.
—Remark on signing the Emancipation Proclamation, January 1, 1863 [RW]

❖

. . . I do order and declare that all persons held as slaves within said designated States, and parts of States, are, and henceforward shall be free; and that the Executive government of the United States, including the military and naval authorities thereof, will recognize and maintain the freedom of said persons.
—Final Emancipation Proclamation, January 1, 1863 [CWBQ]

❖

The colored population is the great *available* and yet *unavailed of* force for restoring the Union. The bare sight of fifty thousand armed and drilled black soldiers on the banks of the Mississippi would end the rebellion at once.
—Letter to Governor of Tennessee Andrew Johnson, March 26, 1863 [HSW]

❖

To sell or enslave any captured person, on account of his color, and for no offence against the laws of war, is a relapse into barbarism and a crime against the civilization of the age. . . .

It is therefore ordered that for every soldier of the United States killed in violation of the laws of war, a rebel soldier shall be executed; and for everyone enslaved by the enemy or sold into slavery, a rebel soldier shall be placed at hard labor on the public works and continued at such labor until the other shall be released and receive the treatment due to a prisoner of war.

—General Orders, Number 252, July 31, 1863 [CW6]

❖

Now, as to pay, we had to make some concessions to prejudice. There were threats that if we made soldiers of them at all, white men would not enlist, would not fight beside them. Besides, it was not believed that a Negro could make a good soldier, as good a soldier as a white man, and hence it was thought that he should not have the same pay as a white man. But I assure you, Mr. Douglass, that in the end they shall have the same pay as white soldiers.

—Remark, on the enlistment of black soldiers, to Frederick Douglass, August 10, 1863 [RW]

❖

You say you will not fight to free negroes. Some of them seem willing to fight for you; but, no matter. Fight you, then, exclusively to save the Union. I issued the proclamation on purpose to aid you in saving the Union.

—Letter to James C. Conkling, August 26, 1863 [HSW]

❖

If slavery is not wrong, nothing is wrong.

—Remarks to Kentucky Governor Thomas Bramlette, *Frankfort Commonwealth* editor Albert Hodges, and Senator Archibald Dixon, March 26, 1864 [CW7]

❖

If we shall suppose that American slavery is one of those offenses which, in the providence of God, must needs come, but which, having continued through His appointed time, He now wills to remove, and that He gives to both North and South this terrible war as the woe due to those by whom the offence came, shall we discern therein any departure from those divine attributes which the believers in a living God always ascribe to Him?

—Second Inaugural Address, March 4, 1865 [HSW]

I have in my lifetime heard many arguments why the negroes ought to be slaves; but if they fight for those who would keep them in slavery it will be a better argument than any I have yet heard. He who will fight for that ought to be a slave. . . . While I have often said that all men ought to be free, yet I would allow those colored persons to be slaves who want to be; and next to them those white persons who argue in favor of making other people slaves. I am in favor of giving an opportunity to such white men to try it on themselves.

—Speech to the 140th Indiana Regiment, on the Confederate Army's plan to enlist slaves, March 17, 1865 [HSW]

STORY-TELLING AND SPEECH-MAKING

I do generally remember a good story when I hear it, but I never did invent anything original; I am only a retail dealer.

—Remark to Noah Brooks (no date) [RW]

❖

Extemporaneous speaking should be practiced and cultivated. It is the lawyer's avenue to the public. However able and faithful he may be in other respects, people are slow to bring him business if he cannot make a speech. And yet there is not a more fatal error to young lawyers than relying too much on speech-making. If anyone, upon his rare powers of speaking, shall claim an exemption from the drudgery of the law, his case is a failure in advance.

—Notes for a lecture on law, c. July 1850 [CW2]

❖

Try to think they're your own words and talk them as you would talk them to me.

—Remark on public-speaking to a Springfield boy,
John Langdon Kaine, c. 1850s [RW]

❖

I am compelled by nature to speak slowly. I commence way back like the boys do when they want to get a good start. My weight and speed get momentum to jump far.

—Remark to William Herndon (no date) [DHD]

❖

It's like the lazy preacher that used to write long sermons, and the explanation was, he got to writin', and was too lazy to stop.

—Remark in court, after a judge wondered at the length of a lawyer's brief,
Bloomington, Illinois, 1854–1855 [LAIKH]

Gentlemen, reading from speeches is a very tedious business, particularly for an old man that has to put on spectacles, and the more so if the man be so tall that he has to bend over to the light.

—Speech, Chicago, July 10, 1858 [CW2]

❖

You don't know what you are talking about, my friend. I am quite willing to answer any gentleman in the crowd who asks an *intelligent* question.

—Answering a heckler during a speech in Chicago, July 10, 1858 [CW2]

❖

Gentlemen, Judge Douglas informed you that this speech of mine was probably carefully prepared. I admit that it was. I am not master of language; I have not a fine education; I am not capable of entering into a disquisition upon dialectics, as I believe you call it; but I do not believe the language I employed bears any such construction as Judge Douglas put upon it. But I don't care about a quibble in regard to words. I know what I meant, and I will not leave this crowd in doubt, if I can explain it to them, what I really meant in the use of that paragraph.

—Speech, Chicago, July 10, 1858 [CW2]

❖

John, it depends a great deal on how you state a case. When Daniel Webster stated a case, it was half-argument. No, you take the subject of predestination; you state it one way, and you cannot make much of it; you state it another, and it seems quite reasonable.

—Remark to John Littlefield, a law student of Lincoln and his partner William Herndon, c. 1859–1860 [LAIKH]

❖

You know that it has not been my custom, since I started on the route to Washington, to make long speeches; I am rather inclined to silence, and whether that be wise or not, it is at least more unusual nowadays to find a man who can hold his tongue than to find one who cannot.

—Speech, Monongahela House, Pittsburgh, Pennsylvania, February 14, 1861 [CW4]

❖

I have made a great many poor speeches in my life, and I feel considerably relieved now to know that the dignity of the position in which I have been placed does not permit me to expose myself any longer. I therefore take shelter, most gladly, in standing back and allowing you to hear speeches from gentlemen who are so very much more able to make them than myself. I thank you for the kindness of your call, but I must keep my word, and not be led into a speech, as I told you I did not appear for that purpose.

—Remarks to New York regiments, Washington, D.C., July 4, 1861 [CW4]

❖

The Secretary of War, you know, holds a pretty tight rein on the Press, so that they shall not tell more than they ought to, and I'm afraid that if I blab too much, he might draw a tight rein on me.

—Speech, Jersey City, New Jersey, at a rail stop while returning to Washington, D. C., from West Point, June 24, 1862 [CW5]

❖

It is very common in this country to find great facility of expression and less common to find great lucidity of thought. The combination of the two in one person is very uncommon; but whenever you do find it, you have a great man.

—Remark to British journalist Edward Dicey, c. 1862–1863 [RW]

❖

It was very kind in Mr. Everett to send me this. I suppose he was afraid I should say something that he wanted to say. He needn't have been alarmed. My speech isn't long.

—Remark to Noah Brooks, on Edward Everett's Gettysburg address, November 14, 1863 [RW]

❖

In my position it is somewhat important that I should not say any foolish things.

A VOICE: If you can help it.

MR. LINCOLN: It very often happens that the only way to help it is to say nothing at all. Believing that is my present condition this evening, I must beg of you to excuse me from addressing you.

—Remarks to his "fellow-citizens" at Gettysburg, Pennsylvania, the day before his Gettysburg Address, November 18, 1863 [CW7]

❖

They say I tell a great many stories. I reckon I do, but I have found in the course of a long experience that common people take them as they run, are more easily influenced and informed through the medium of a broad illustration than in any other way, and as to what the hypercritical few may think, I don't care. . . . I have originated but two stories in my life, but I tell tolerably well other people's stories.

—Remark to Chauncey Depew of New York, 1864 [RW]

❖

When quite young, at school, Daniel was one day guilty of a gross violation of the rules. He was detected in the act and called up by the teacher for punishment. This was to be the old-fashioned "feruling" of the hand. His hands happened to be very dirty. Knowing this, on his way to the teacher's desk he spit upon the palm of his right hand, wiping it off upon the side of his pantaloons. "Give me your hand, sir," said the teacher, very sternly. Out went the right hand, partly cleansed. The teacher looked at it a moment, and said, "Daniel, if you will find another hand in this schoolroom as filthy as that, I will let you off this time." Instantly from behind his back came the left hand. "Here it is, sir," was the ready reply. "That will do," said the teacher, "for this time; you can take your seat sir!"

—Anecdote, retelling a story about Daniel Webster, May 31, 1864 [RW]

❖

I cannot frame a toast to Burns. I can say nothing worthy of his generous heart and transcending genius. Thinking of what he has said, I cannot say anything which seems worth saying.

—Note to himself on being asked for a sentiment on the 106th birthday of the poet Robert Burns, January 25, 1865 [CW8]

❖

Well, for those who like that sort of thing, I should think it is just the sort of thing they would like.

—Remark to an author who had read him a manuscript on "an abstruse subject" (no date) [ALL]

❖

Well, there are two ways of relating a story. If you have an auditor who has the time and is inclined to listen, lengthen it out, pour it out slowly as if from a jug. If you have a poor listener, hasten it, shorten it, shoot it out of a popgun.

—Remark to the pastor Phineas Gurney (no date) [RW]

THE WAR AND HIS GENERALS

The rebels attack Fort Sumter, and your citizens attack troops sent to the defense of the Government and the lives and property in Washington, and yet you would have me break my oath and surrender the Government without a blow. There is no Washington in that—no Jackson in that—no manhood nor honor in that.

—Remarks to a YMCA committee from Baltimore, April 22, 1861 [CW4]

❖

I have no desire to invade the South; but I must have troops to defend this Capital. Geographically it lies surrounded by the soil of Maryland; and mathematically the necessity exists that they should come over her territory. Our men are not moles, and can't dig under the earth; they are not birds, and can't fly through the air. There is no way but to march across, and that they must do. But in doing this there is no need of collision. Keep your rowdies in Baltimore, and there will be no bloodshed. Go home and tell your people that if they will not attack us, we will not attack them; but if they do attack us, we will return it, and that severely.

—Remarks to a YMCA committee from Baltimore, April 22, 1861 [CW4]

❖

The people of Virginia have thus allowed this giant insurrection to make its nest within her borders; and this government has no choice left but to deal with it *where* it finds it.

—Message to Congress in Special Session, July 4, 1861 [GS]

❖

Have you noticed the facts that less than one half-day's cost of this war would pay for all the slaves in Delaware, at four hundred dollars per head?—that eighty-seven days' cost of this war would pay for all in Delaware, Maryland, District of Columbia, Kentucky, and Missouri at the same price? Were those States to take the step, do you doubt that it would shorten the war more than eighty-seven days, and thus be an actual saving of expense. Please look at these things, and consider whether there should not be another article in the *Times*?

—Letter to Henry Raymond, March 9, 1862 [CW5]

❖

I expect to maintain this contest until successful, or till I die, or am conquered, or my term expires, or Congress or the country forsakes me; and I would publicly appeal to the country for this new force were it not that I fear a general panic and stampede would follow—so hard is it to have a thing understood as it really is. I think the new force should be all, or nearly all, infantry, principally because such can be raised most cheaply and quickly.

—Letter to William Steward, June 28, 1862 [CW5]

❖

Broken eggs cannot be mended; but Louisiana has nothing to do now but to take her place in the Union as it was, barring the already broken eggs. The sooner she does so, the smaller will be the amount of that which will be past mending. This government cannot much longer play a game in which it stakes all, and its enemies stake nothing. Those enemies must understand that they cannot experiment for ten years trying to destroy the government, and if they fail, still come back into the Union unhurt. If they expect in any contingency to ever have the Union as it was, I join with the writer in saying, "Now is the time."

—Letter to August Belmont, July 31, 1862 [CW5]

❖

Doesn't it strike you as queer that I, who couldn't cut the head off of a chicken, and who was sick at the sight of blood, should be cast into the middle of a great war, with blood flowing all about me?

—Remark, (no date) [DHD]

❖

The will of God prevails. In great contests each party claims to act in accordance with the will of God. Both *may* be, and one *must* be, wrong. God cannot be *for* and *against* the same thing at the same time. In the present civil war it is quite possible that God's purpose is something different from the purpose of either party—and yet the human instrumentalities, working just as they do, are of the best adaptation to effect His purpose.

—"Meditation on the Divine Will," c. September 2, 1862 [CWBQ]

I am almost ready to say . . . that God wills this contest, and wills that it shall not end yet.
>   —"Meditation on the Divine Will," c. September 2, 1862 [CW5]

❖

I sincerely wish war was an easier and pleasanter business than it is; but it does not admit of holidays.
>   —Remark to Thomas H. Clay, asking for his army division's reassignment
>   to Kentucky, c. September 1862 [CW5]

❖

If I had had my way, this war would never have been commenced; if I had been allowed my way this war would have ended before this, but we find it still continues; and we must believe that He permits it for some wise purpose of his own, mysterious and unknown to us; and though with our limited understandings we may not be able to comprehend it, yet we cannot but believe that He who made the world still governs it.
>   —Letter to Eliza Gurney, October 26, 1862 [CW5]

❖

So this is the little lady who made this big war?
>   —Remark to the author of *Uncle Tom's Cabin,* Harriet Beecher Stowe,
>   November 1862 [LAIKH]

❖

Whichever way it ends, I have the impression that I shan't last long after it's over.
>   —Remark to author Harriet Beecher Stowe, November 1862 [LAIKH]

❖

We are like whalers who have been on a long chase. We have at last got the harpoon into the monster, but we must look now how we steer, or with one flop of his tail he will send us all into eternity.
>   —Remark to New York Governor Edwin Morgan, January 1863 [CWBQ]

❖

I do not think the people of Pennsylvania should be uneasy about an invasion. Doubtless a small force of the enemy is flourishing about in the Northern part of Virginia on the "screw-horn" principle, on purpose to divert us in another quarter. I believe it is nothing more. We think we have adequate forces close after them.

—Letter to Governor Andrew Curtin of Pennsylvania, April 28, 1863. (Two months later the Confederates invaded southern Pennsylvania, and the Union forces met and defeated them at Gettysburg.) [CW6]

❖

The rebellion thus begun soon ran into the present civil war; and, in certain respects, it began on very unequal terms between the parties. The insurgents had been preparing for it more than thirty years, while the government had taken no steps to resist them.

—Letter to Erastus Corning and others, June 12, 1863 [HSW]

❖

I cannot be shut up in an iron cage and guarded. If I have business at the War Office, I must take my hat and go there, and if to kill me is within the purposes of this rebellion, no precaution can prevent it. You may guard me at a single point, but I will necessarily be exposed at others. People come to see me every day and I receive them, and I do not know but that some of them are secessionists or engaged in plots to kill me. The truth is, if any man has made up his mind that he will give his life for mine, he can take mine.

—Remark to Leonard Swett, summer 1863 [RW]

❖

We have certain information that Vicksburg surrendered to General Grant on the 4th of July. Now, if General Meade can complete his work, so gloriously prosecuted thus far, by the literal or substantial destruction of Lee's army, the rebellion will be over.

—Letter to Major General Henry Halleck, on the battle of Gettysburg and its aftermath, July 7, 1863 [CW6]

❖

My belief is that the permanent estimate of what a general does in the field is fixed by the "cloud of witnesses" who have been with him in the field; and that relying on these, he who has the right needs not to fear.

—Letter to Major General John McClernand, August 12, 1863 [CW6]

❖

There are those who are dissatisfied with me. To such I would say: You desire peace; and you blame me that we do not have it. But how can we attain it? There are but three conceivable ways. First, to suppress the rebellion by force of arms. This, I am trying to do. Are you for it? If you are, so far we are agreed. If you are not for it, a second way is, to give up the Union. I am against this. Are you for it? If you are, you should say so plainly. If you are not for force, nor yet for *dissolution*, there only remains some unimaginable *compromise*. I do not believe any compromise embracing the maintenance of the Union is now possible. All I learn leads to a directly opposite belief. The strength of the rebellion is its military—its army. That army dominates all the country and all the people within its range. Any offer of terms made by any man or men within that range, in opposition to that army, is simply nothing for the present; because such man or men have no power whatever to enforce their side of a compromise, if one were made with them.

—Letter to James C. Conkling, August 26, 1863 [HSW]

❖

You are a farmer, I believe; if not, you will understand me. Suppose you had a large cattle yard full of all sorts of cattle, cows, oxen, and bulls, and you kept selling and killing your cows and oxen, taking good care of your bulls, By and by you would find out you had nothing but a yard full of old bulls, good for nothing under heaven. Now it will be just so with my army if I don't stop making brigadier generals.

—Remark to a man soliciting another's promotion, September 14, 1863 [RW]

❖

If the enemy's sixty thousand are sufficient to keep our ninety thousand away from Richmond, why, by the same rule, may not forty thousand of ours keep their sixty thousand away from Washington, leaving us fifty thousand to put to some other use? Having practically come to the mere defensive, it seems to be no economy at all to employ twice as many men for that object as are needed.

—Letter to General Henry Halleck, September 19, 1863 [HSW]

❖

The restoration of the Rebel States to the Union must rest upon the principle of civil and political equality of both races; and it must be sealed by general amnesty.

—Letter to James Wadsworth, c. January 1864 [CW7]

❖

When the war began three years ago, neither party, nor any man, expected it would last till now. Each looked for the end, in some way, long ere today. Neither did any anticipate that domestic slavery would be much affected by the war. But here we are; the war has not ended, and

slavery has been much affected—how much needs not now to be recounted. So true it is that man proposes, and God disposes.
—Speech, Sanitary Fair, Baltimore, Maryland, April 18, 1864 [HSW]

❖

War, at the best, is terrible, and this war of ours, in its magnitude and in its duration, is one of the most terrible. It has deranged business, totally in many localities, and partially in all localities. It has destroyed property and ruined homes; it has produced a national debt and taxation unprecedented, at least in this country. It has carried mourning to almost every home, until it can almost be said that the "heavens are hung in black."
—Speech, Great Central Sanitary Fair, Philadelphia, June 16, 1864 [HSW]

❖

We accepted this war for an object, a worthy object, and the war will end when that object is attained. Under God, I hope it never will end until that time. Speaking of the present campaign, General Grant is reported to have said, "I am going through on this line if it takes all summer." This war has taken three years; it was begun or accepted upon the line of restoring the national authority over the whole national domain, and for the American people, as far as my knowledge enables me to speak, I say we are going through on this line if it takes three years more.
—Speech, Great Central Sanitary Fair, Philadelphia, June 16, 1864 [HSW]

❖

I am sure you would not desire me to say, or to leave an inference, that I am ready, whenever convenient, to join in re-enslaving those who shall have served us in consideration of our promise. As matter of morals, could such treachery by any possibility escape the curses of Heaven, or of any good man? As matter of policy, to *announce* such a purpose would ruin the Union cause itself. All recruiting of colored men would instantly cease, and all colored men now in our service would instantly desert us. And rightfully too. Why should they give their lives for us with full notice of our purpose to betray them?
—Letter to Charles D. Robinson, August 17, 1864 [CW7]

❖

Abandon all the posts now possessed by black men, surrender all these advantages to the enemy, and we would be compelled to abandon the war in three weeks.
—Remark to Alexander Randall and Joseph Mills, August 19, 1864 [CW7]

My enemies say I am now carrying on this war for the sole purpose of abolition. It is and will be carried on so long as I am President for the sole purpose of restoring the Union. But no human power can subdue this rebellion without using the Emancipation lever as I have done. Freedom has given us the control of 200,000 able-bodied men, born and raised on Southern soil. It will give us more yet. Just so much it has subtracted from the strength of our enemies, and instead of alienating the South from us, there evidences of a fraternal feeling growing up between our own and rebel soldiers. My enemies condemn my emancipation policy. Let them prove by the history of this war that we can restore the Union without it.

—Remarks to Alexander Randall and Joseph Mills, August 19, 1864 [CW7]

❖

Much is being said about peace; and no man desires peace more ardently than I. Still, I am yet unprepared to give up the Union for a peace which, so achieved, could not be of much duration. The preservation of our Union was *not* the sole avowed object for which the war was commenced. It was commenced for precisely the reverse object—to destroy our Union. The insurgents commenced it by firing upon the Star of the West, and on Fort Sumter, and by other similar acts.

—Letter to Isaac Schermerhorn, September 12, 1864 [CW8]

❖

I wish all men to be free. I wish the material prosperity of the already free which I feel sure the extinction of slavery would bring. I wish to see, in process of disappearing, that only thing which ever could bring this nation to civil war.

—Letter to Henry Hoffman, October 10, 1864 [CW8]

❖

I feel how weak and fruitless must be any words of mine which should attempt to beguile you from the grief of a loss so overwhelming. But I cannot refrain from tendering to you the consolation that may be found in the thanks of the Republic they died to save.

—Letter to Mrs. Lydia Bixby, the mother of two sons killed in battle (not five as Lincoln believed), November 21, 1864 [CWBQ]

❖

In stating a single condition of peace, I mean simply to say that the war will cease on the part of the government whenever it shall have ceased on the part of those who began it.

—Annual message to Congress, December 6, 1864 [HSW]

Both parties deprecated war; but one of them would make war rather than let the nation survive; and the other would accept war rather than let it perish. And the war came.

—Second Inaugural Address, March 4, 1865 [HSW]

❖

With malice toward none; with charity for all; with firmness in the right, as God gives us to see the right, let us strive on to finish the work we are in; to bind up the nation's wounds; to care for him who shall have borne the battle, and for his widow, and his orphan—to do all which may achieve and cherish a just and lasting peace, among ourselves, and with all nations.

—Second Inaugural Address, March 4, 1865 [HSW]

❖

I expect it to wear as well as—perhaps better than—anything I have produced; but I believe it is not immediately popular. Men are not flattered by being shown that there has been a difference of purpose between the Almighty and them. To deny it, however, in this case, is to deny that there is a God governing the world. It is a truth which I thought needed to be told; and as whatever of humiliation there is in it falls most directly on myself, I thought others might afford for me to tell it.

—Letter to Thurlow Weed, on the reception of Lincoln's second inaugural address, March 15, 1865 [HSW]

❖

The pilots on our Western rivers steer from *point to point* as they call it—setting the course of the boat no farther than they can see; and that is all I propose to myself in this great problem.

—Remark to James G. Blaine, on his reconstruction policy (no date) [DHD]

❖

Get them to plowing once and gathering in their own little crops, eating popcorn at their own firesides, and you can't get them to shoulder a musket again for half a century.

—Remark on his reconstruction policy to Admiral David Porter, late March, 1865 [RW]

My God, my God! Can't you spare more effusions of blood? We have had so much of it.

> —In conversation with Generals Grant and Sherman,
> on board the *River Queen,* when they told the President
> that Confederate General Robert E. Lee might have his Army
> of Northern Virginia fight one last battle, March 28, 1865 [CWBQ]

❖

Thank God I have lived to see this. It seems to me that I have been dreaming a horrid dream for four years, and now the nightmare is gone.

> —Remark to Admiral David Porter, at the Union base on
> the James River, Virginia, April 3, 1865 [CWBQ]

❖

General Sheridan says, "If the thing is pressed I think that Lee will surrender." Let the *thing* be pressed.

> —Letter to Lt. General Ulysses S. Grant, April 7, 1865 [CW8]

❖

The evacuation of Petersburg and Richmond, and the surrender of the principal insurgent army, give hope of a righteous and speedy peace whose joyous expression cannot be restrained.

> —Last speech, from a White House balcony, April 11, 1865 [CW8]

HIS GENERALS

Ulysses S. Grant

I can't spare this man; he fights!

> —Remark to Colonel Alexander McClure, who had urged the President to
> remove Grant from his command after the battle of Shiloh, April 1862 [YS]

❖

What I want, and what the people want, is generals who will fight battles and win victories. Grant has done this, and I propose to stand by him.

> —Remark to General John Thayer, in the midst of the outcry
> against Grant, c. April 1862 [CWBQ]

❖

So Grant gets drunk, does he? . . . Well, you needn't waste your time getting proof; you just find out, to oblige me, what brand of whiskey Grant drinks, because I want to send a barrel of it to each one of my generals.

> —Remark to Grant's "particularly active detractors"; Grant, "at that period,
> was inflicting heavy damage upon the Confederates" (no date) [YS]

Whether General Grant shall or shall not consummate the capture of
Vicksburg, his campaign from the beginning of this month up to the
twenty-second day of it is one of the most brilliant in the world.
                              —Letter to Isaac N. Arnold, May 26, 1863 [HSW]

❖

If this Army of the Potomac was good for anything—if the officers had
anything in them—if the army had any legs, they could move thirty
thousand men down to Lynchburg and catch Longstreet. Can anybody
doubt if Grant were here in command that he would catch him?
                 —Remark to his secretary John Nicolay, December 7, 1863 [DHD]

❖

Grant is the first general I've had. He's a general! . . . You know how it's
been with all the rest. As soon as I put a man in command of the army,
he'd come to me with a plan of campaign and about as much as say,
"Now, I don't believe I can do it, but if you say so, I'll try it on," and so
put the responsibility of success or failure on me. They all wanted me to
be the general. Now, it isn't so with Grant. . . . He doesn't ask me to do
impossibilities for him, and he's the first general I've had that didn't!
                    —Remark to the journalist William O. Stoddard (no date) [RW]

❖

The nation's appreciation of what you have done, and its reliance upon
you for what remains to do, in the existing great struggle, are now presented with this commission constituting you Lieutenant General in the
Army of the United States. With this high honor devolves upon you also
a corresponding responsibility. As the country herein trusts you, so, under
God, it will sustain you.
              —Speech presenting Grant with his commission as Lieutenant General,
                       in the President's Cabinet chamber, March 9, 1864 [CW7]

❖

You and I, Mr. Stanton, have been trying to boss this job, and we have
not succeeded very well with it. We have sent across the mountains for
Mr. Grant, as Mrs. Grant calls him, to relieve us, and I think we had better leave him alone to do as he pleases.
                    —Remark to Secretary of War Edwin Stanton (no date) [DHD]

❖

Not expecting to see you again before the Spring campaign opens, I wish
to express, in this way, my entire satisfaction with what you have done up
to this time, so far as I understand it. The particulars of your plans I nei-

ther know nor seek to know. You are vigilant and self-reliant; and, pleased with this, I wish not to obtrude any restraints or constraints upon you. While I am very anxious that any great disaster, or capture of our men in great numbers, shall be avoided, I know that these points are less likely to escape your attention than they would mine.

> —Letter to Grant, at Army Headquarters, Culpeper Court-House,
> Virginia, April 30, 1864 [HSW]

❖

I have seen your dispatch expressing your unwillingness to break your hold where you are. Neither am I willing. Hold on with a bulldog grip, and chew and choke as much as possible.

> —Telegram to Grant, August 17, 1864. (Reading this, Grant observed to staff
> members, "The President has more nerve than any of his advisers.") [CWBQ]

Joseph Hooker

I have placed you at the head of the Army of the Potomac. Of course I have done this upon what appear to me to be sufficient reasons. And yet I think it best for you to know that there are some things in regard to which, I am not quite satisfied with you. I believe you to be a brave and skilled soldier, which, of course, I like. I also believe you do not mix politics and your profession, in which you are right. You have confidence in yourself, which is a valuable, if not an indispensable quality. You are ambitious, which, within reasonable bounds, does good rather than harm. But I think that during General Burnside's command of the Army, you have taken counsel of your ambition, and thwarted him as much as you could, in which you did a great wrong to the country, and to a most meritorious and honorable brother officer. I have heard, in such way as to believe it, of your recently saying that both the Army and the Government needed a Dictator. Of course it was not for this, but in spite of it, that I have given you the command. . . .

And now, beware of rashness, but with energy and sleepless vigilance go forward and give us victories.

> —Letter to Hooker, giving him command of the Army of the Potomac,
> January 26, 1863 [CW6]

❖

Have you already in your mind a plan wholly or partially formed? If you have, prosecute it without interference from me. If you have not, please inform me, so that I, incompetent as I may be, can try to assist in the formation of some plan for the Army.

> —Letter to Hooker, May 7, 1863 [CW6]

In one word, I would not take any risk of being entangled upon the river, like an ox jumped half over a fence, and liable to be torn by dogs, front and rear, without a fair chance to gore one way or kick the other. If Lee would come to my side of the river, I would keep on the same side and fight him, or act on the defense, according as might be my estimate of his strength relatively to my own.

—Letter to Hooker, June 5, 1863 [HSW]

❖

I think Lee's Army, and not *Richmond*, is your true objective point. . . . Fight him when opportunity offers. If he stays where he is, fret him, and fret him.

—Telegram to Hooker, June 10, 1863. (Lee's Army of Northern Virginia had begun its invasion campaign, and Hooker, feeling helpless to stop the invasion, saw on the other hand an opportunity to take Richmond.) [CW6]

❖

If the head of Lee's army is at Martinsburg and the tail of it on the plank road between Fredericksburg and Chancellorsville, the animal must be very slim somewhere. Could you not break him?

—Telegram to Hooker, June 14, 1863 [HSW]

George B. McClellan

I will hold McClellan's horse if he will only bring us success.

—Remark on McClellan's deliberate rudeness to him when Lincoln paid him a call, November 13, 1861 [CWBQ]

❖

Why in tarnation . . . couldn't the general have known whether a boat would go through that lock before he spent a million dollars getting them there? I am no engineer, but it seems to me that if I wished to know whether a boat would go through a . . . lock, common sense would teach me to go and measure it. I am almost despairing at these results.

—Remark to General Randolph Marcy, McClellan's father-in-law, on McClellan's plan to send boats up a Potomac River canal, February 27, 1862 [DHD]

❖

. . . once more let me tell you, it is indispensable to *you* that you strike a blow. I am powerless to help this. You will do me the justice to remember I always insisted that going down the Bay in search of a field, instead of fighting at or near Manassas, was only shifting, and not surmounting, a difficulty—that we would find the same enemy and the same or equal intrenchments at either place. The country will not fail to note—is now noting—that the present hesitation to move upon an intrenched enemy is but the story of Manassas repeated.

I beg to assure you that I have never written you, or spoken to you, in greater kindness of feeling than now, nor with a fuller purpose to sustain you, so far as in my most anxious judgment I consistently can. *But you must act.*

—Letter to McClellan, April 9, 1862 [CW5]

❖

I think the time is near when you must either attack Richmond or give up the job and come to the defense of Washington.

—Letter to McClellan, May 25, 1862 [CWBQ]

❖

Save your army at all events. Will send reinforcements as fast as we can. Of course they cannot reach you today, tomorrow, or next day. I have not said you were ungenerous for saying you needed reinforcement. I thought you were ungenerous in assuming that I did not send them as fast as I could. I feel any misfortune to you and your army quite as keenly as you feel it yourself.

—Letter to McClellan, June 28, 1862 [CW5]

❖

If, in your frequent mention of responsibility, you have the impression that I blame you for not doing more than you can, please be relieved of such impression. I only beg that in like manner you will not ask impossibilities of me. If you think you are not strong enough to take Richmond just now, I do not ask you to try just now. Save the Army, material and personnel; and I will strengthen it for the offensive again, as fast as I can.

—Letter to McClellan, July 2, 1862 [HSW]

❖

Three times round and out is the rule in baseball. Stuart has been round twice around McClellan. The third time, by the rules of the game, he must surrender.

—Remark to Adams S. Hill, of the *New York Tribune,* on Confederate
General J. E. B. Stuart, who had twice led his cavalry around
McClellan's Army of the Potomac, October 1862 [CWBQ]

You remember my speaking to you of what I called your overcautious-
ness. Are you not overcautious when you assume that you cannot do
what the enemy is constantly doing? Should you not claim to be at least
his equal in prowess, and act upon the claim?

—Letter to McClellan, October 13, 1862. (Lincoln urged McClellan
to appreciate his army's advantages after the battle of Antietam
and immediately attack.) [CWBQ]

❖

I have just read your dispatch about sore-tongued and fatigued horses.
Will you pardon me for asking what the horses of your army have done
since the battle of Antietam that fatigue anything?

—Telegram to McClellan, October 25, 1862. (Two days later Lincoln
apologized in a letter and explained his impatience with
"five weeks of total inaction of the Army.") [CWBQ]

❖

I said I would remove him if he let Lee's army get away from him, and I
must do so. He has got the "slows," Mr. Blair.

—Remark to General Francis Blair, on McClellan,
November 7, 1862 [CWBQ]

❖

By direction of the President of the United States, it is ordered that
Major General McClellan be relieved from the command of the Army
of the Potomac, and that Major General Burnside take the command of
that army.

—Orders to Major General Henry Halleck, which McClellan received
November 7, 1862 [CWBQ]

George G. Meade

They will be ready to fight a magnificent battle when there is no enemy
there to fight.

—Remark after reading Meade's telegraph message that
the Army of the Potomac, having won at Gettysburg,
would not be ready to attack Confederate General Robert E. Lee's
fleeing army until the next day, July 12, 1863 [CWBQ]

Again, my dear general, I do not believe you appreciate the magnitude of the misfortune involved in Lee's escape. He was within your easy grasp, and to have closed upon him would, in connection with our other late successes, have ended the war. As it is, the war will be prolonged indefinitely. . . . Your golden opportunity is gone, and I am distressed immeasurably because of it.

> —Letter, never sent, to Meade, July 14, 1863 [HSW]

❖

Our army held the war in the hollow of their hand, and they would not close it. We had gone through all the labor of tilling and planting an enormous crop, and when it was ripe we did not harvest it. Still, I am very grateful to Meade for the great service he did at Gettysburg.

> —In conversation with his assistant private secretary, John Hay,
> July 19, 1863 [CWBQ]

❖

Do you know, General, what your attitude toward Lee for a week after the battle reminded me of? . . . I'll be hanged if I could think of anything else than an old woman trying to shoo her geese across a creek.

> —Remark to Meade on his lack of pursuit of Lee's Army
> of Northern Virginia, which, after Gettysburg, escaped across
> the Potomac, October 23, 1863 [CWBQ]

William S. Rosecrans

Truth to speak, I do not appreciate this matter of rank on paper, as you officers do. The world will not forget that you fought the battle of Stones River and it will never care a fig whether you rank General Grant on paper or he so ranks you.

> —Letter to Rosecrans, March 17, 1863 [CW6]

❖

He is confused and stunned, like a duck hit on the head, ever since Chickamauga.

> —Remark to his secretary, John Hay, on Rosecrans,
> October 24, 1863. (Lincoln removed Rosecrans from his command
> of the Army of the Cumberland on October 19.) [CWBQ]

Philip H. Sheridan

. . . how fortunate for the Secesh that Sheridan was a very little man. If he had been a large man, there is no knowing what he would have done with them.

> —Response to a serenade from a crowd celebrating Sheridan for his cavalry's series of victories in September and October, October 21, 1864 [CW8]

❖

This Sheridan is a little Irishman, but he is a big fighter.

> —Remark to Annie Wittenmyer (no date) [RW]

❖

General Sheridan, when this peculiar war began I thought a cavalryman should be at least six feet four inches high, but I have changed my mind. Five feet four will do in a pinch.

> —Remark to Sheridan, after his successful cavalry raid in northern Virginia, March 26, 1865 [CWBQ]

William Tecumseh Sherman

I know what hole he went in at, but I can't tell what hole he will come out of.

> —Remark to Major General William T. Sherman's brother, Senator John Sherman of Ohio, on the general's march through Georgia, early December, 1864 [RW]

❖

The most interesting news we now have is from Sherman. We all know where he went in at, but I can't tell where he will come out at.

> —Response to a serenade from "friends and fellow citizens," on Sherman's march through Georgia, December 6, 1864 [CW8]

❖

Many, many thanks for your Christmas gift—the capture of Savannah.

> —Letter to Sherman, December 26, 1864 [HSW]

❖

A man once had taken the total abstinence pledge. When visiting a friend, he was invited to take a drink, but he declined, on the score of his pledge, when his friend suggested lemonade, which was accepted. In preparing the lemonade, the friend pointed to the brandy bottle, and said the lemonade would be more palatable if he were to pour in a little brandy; when his guest said, if he could do "unbeknown" to him, he would not object.

> —Remark to Major Generals Ulysses S. Grant and William Tecumseh Sherman, answering Sherman's question of what was to be done with Confederate President Jefferson Davis when he was captured; "from which illustration," writes Sherman, "I inferred that Mr. Lincoln wanted Davis to escape, 'unbeknown' to him, and 'clear out' of the country, and the men composing the Confederate armies [to go] back to their homes, at work on their farms and shops," March 28, 1865 [LAIKH]

WOMEN AND MARRIAGE

Whatever woman may cast her lot with mine, should any ever do so, it is my intention to do all in my power to make her happy and contented; and there is nothing I can imagine that would make me more unhappy than to fail in the effort.

—Letter to his fiancee Mary Owens, May 7, 1837 [CW1]

❖

If you feel yourself in any degree bound to me, I am now willing to release you, provided you wish it; while, on the other hand, I am willing, and even anxious, to bind you faster, if I can be convinced that it will, in any considerable degree, add to your happiness. This, indeed, is the whole question with me. Nothing would make me more miserable than to believe you miserable—nothing more unhappy than to know you were so.

—Letter to Mary Owens, August 16, 1837 [CW1]

❖

Others have been made fools of by the girls; but this can never with truth be said of me. I most emphatically, in this instance, made a fool of myself. I have now come to the conclusion never again to think of marrying, and for this reason; I can never be satisfied with anyone who would be block-head enough to have me.

—Letter to his friend Mrs. Eliza Browning, on his failed engagement to Mary Owens, April 1, 1838 [HSW]

❖

I am now the most miserable man living. If what I feel were equally distributed to the whole human family, there would not be one cheerful face on the earth.

—Letter to John T. Stuart, on Lincoln's broken engagement with Mary Todd, who later, in any case, became his wife, January 23, 1841 [HSW]

Nothing new here, except my marrying, which to me is a matter of profound wonder.

> —Letter to Samuel D. Marshall, November 11, 1842. (Lincoln married Mary Todd on November 4.) [HSW]

❖

In this troublesome world, we are never quite satisfied. When you were here, I thought you hindered me some in attending to business; but now, having nothing but business—no variety—it has grown exceedingly tasteless to me. I hate to sit down and direct documents, and I hate to stay in this old room by myself.

> —Letter to his wife Mary, from Washington, D.C., where he was serving as a Congressman, April 16, 1848 [CW1]

❖

With pleasure I write my name in your album. Ere long some younger man will be more happy to confer *his* name upon *you*. Don't allow it, Mary, until fully assured that he is worthy of the happiness.

> —Note, autograph book of Mary Delahay, December 7, 1859 [HSW]

❖

Your kind congratulatory letter, of August, was received in due course—and should have been answered sooner. The truth is I have never corresponded much with ladies; and hence I postpone writing letters to them, as a business which I do not understand. I can only say now I thank you for the good opinion you express of me, fearing, at the same time, I may not be able to maintain it through life.

> —Letter to Mrs. M. J. Green, September 22, 1860 [CW4]

❖

So this is the little lady that all us folks in Washington like so much. Don't you ever come 'round here asking me to do some of those impossible things you women always ask for, for I would have to do it, and then I'd get into trouble.

> —Remark to the actress Rose Eytinge (no date) [RW]

❖

If you knew how little harm it does me and how much good it does her, you wouldn't wonder that I am meek.

> —Remark to friends, on his wife Mary's having had her way in an argument, 1865 [RW]